Burros and Paintbrushes

A WARDLAW BOOK

Going Home from Market

BURROS AND PAINTBRUSHES

A Mexican Adventure

Written and Illustrated by

EVERETT GEE JACKSON

TEXAS A&M UNIVERSITY PRESS

COLLEGE STATION

Library of Congress Cataloging in Publication Data

Jackson, Everett Gee, 1900–
 Burros and paintbrushes.

 "A Wardlaw book."
 1. Mexico—Social life and customs. 2. Jackson,
Everett Gee, 1900–   . 3. Artists—United States—
Biography. 4. Artists—Mexico—Biography. I. Title.
II. Series.
F1234.J26 1985   972.08'23'0924   84-40558
ISBN 0-89096-229-4

Manufactured in the United States of America
FIRST EDITION

To my three sweethearts, Eileen, Jerry Gee, and Hildy

Contents

Color Plates

Preface

When I was five or six years old, the Battle of the Alamo was fought on the playground of my school. The entire grammar school took part in that battle, and I was given the role of a Texan who got shot in the very first skirmish. I was told by my teacher to lie down and play dead as soon as the battle started, which I did. So I didn't get to see much of what went on, but it made a deep impression on me, and I knew for years afterwards that I had been killed by a Mexican. The fact that I had not only taken part in the Battle of the Alamo, but had also died there, along with Jim Bowie and Davy Crockett, made it inevitable that I would someday go to Mexico and see for myself the kind of people who had done me in.

In my hometown, Mexia, Texas, there was only one Mexican. His name was Martínez, and he made and sold, up and down the streets, the most delicious tamales, the small kind some people call "Texas tamales." I had a great fear of—but also admiration for—this man, Martínez. When I would hear him coming down the street yelling "ta-MAL-es," I would run and tell my mother, hoping she would buy some of his wares. But I would also make sure to stay out of sight, for I did not want to get killed by a Mexican again.

One day, as my mother and I were walking to town along the sidewalk, we met this Martínez with his box of tamales. Inside the square box, which he carried by a strap over his shoulder, was a five-gallon can with a lid.

When Martínez would lift that lid, the steam and the magic odor would fill the air. On this occasion, feeling fairly safe with my mother, I reached around and touched the bright red bag he used as a cover for his box. When I did that, old Martínez gave my hand a slap. That was too much. I simply wet my britches from fright. No longer could there be any doubt where my major interest in life would lie.

Many people have wondered why I spend so much time in Mexico, why I go back again and again, why I even carried my bride there and returned so many times wih her that she finally asked if there were any other place in the world we might someday visit. Since I had become a painter and illustrator of books, people assumed that for some reason I preferred Mexican subject matter. It is true that from the beginning I found beauty wherever I went in that country. But this is the first time I have revealed the true psychological reason for my searches from one end of that land to the other: subconsciously, I have been trying to find out all I could about those people who killed me in the Battle of the Alamo.

This project has proved to be without end.

There is no "Mexico." There are many, many Mexicos, and as many Mexicans who may have shot me at the Alamo as there are inhabitants in that land that reaches all the way to the Guatemalan border.

I have often suspected that the Mexican I was searching for was the one who suddenly stops singing and starts yelping in those Mexican orchestras called mariachis. But then when I have listened to him yelp like a coyote, I have known that he would not have wanted to shoot me, and that he would never have done it unless he was out of his mind with too much tequila.

Once while wading in a little stream that empties into the Río Grande on the Mexican side of the border, miles away from people, I suddenly knew that I was being looked at from a cliff above. I did not look up for a long time while I was being looked at. It was a bright, sunny afternoon, and a day of still silence. Suddenly I looked up and saw that I had been watched by a coyote, which immediately disappeared.

Another time, not long after that, I was riding over a flat plain to the west of the San Rodrigo River. A few hundred yards away, a dead cow was stretched out all alone on the prairie. Not even a bush or a cactus was nearby. Then suddenly I saw a coyote come up to that cow and go inside its carcass. I went over and examined the cow, expecting to see the coyote come out and run away. I even turned the carcass over. But there was no coyote there.

That is the way my search has always been.

This book is about the early years of that search, when I first began to explore Mexico, in the 1920's. The one called "Lowelito" in this story was Lowell Houser, from Ames, Iowa. His father was a streetcar conductor in Ames, and his brother was chairman of the board of Sears Roebuck. Our Mexican friends in Chapala started calling Lowell "Lowelito," and that name stuck to him.

Lowelito and I became friends in 1920, when we both were studying at the Art Institute of Chicago. That was a few years before I discovered Eileen in San Diego, California, where to this day she is well known and highly regarded. On our first trip to Mexico, Lowelito

and I went up into the mountains of the state of Coahuila and lived there for a while near a tribe of Kickapoo Indians. Finally, in 1923, we arrived in Guadalajara,
where we drew and painted for several weeks before we
found Chapala. This story starts in Guadalajara at that
time, and covers four years of living and painting in
Mexico.

Publisher's Acknowledgment

The Texas A&M University Press is privileged to add its imprint to this Wardlaw Book. The designation claims a special place in the list of Texas A&M publications.

Supported with funds inspired by the initiative of Chester Kerr, former head of Yale University Press, this book, along with its companion volumes, perpetuates the association of Frank H. Wardlaw's name with a select group of titles appropriate to his reputation as man of letters, distinguished publisher, and founder of three university presses.

Donors of these funds represent a wide cross-section of Frank Wardlaw's admirers, including colleagues from scholarly presses throughout the country as well as those from other callings who recognize and applaud the many contributions that he has made to scholarship, literature, and publishing in his four decades of active service.

The Texas A&M University Press acknowledges with profound appreciation these donors.

Mr. Herbert S. Bailey, Jr.
Mr. Robert Barnes
Mr. W. Walker Cowan
Mr. John Ervin, Jr.
Mr. William D. Fitch
Mr. August Frugé
Mr. David H. Gilbert
Mr. Kenneth Johnson

Mr. Chester Kerr
Mr. Robert T. King
Mr. Carl C. Krueger, Jr.
Mr. John H. Kyle
Mrs. S. M. McAshan, Jr.
Mr. Kenneth E. Montague
Mr. Edward J. Mosher
Mrs. Florence Rosengren

Burros and Paintbrushes

1
Chapala

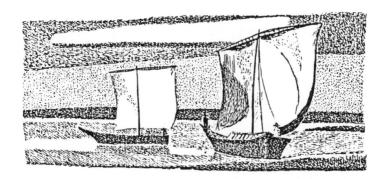

When Lowelito and I arrived in Guadalajara, by train from Querétaro, in 1923, we were surprised and puzzled to hear that the train just preceding our own had been stopped by bandits. We were told that all the Americans on the train had been taken off near Ocotlán and shot. Lowelito and I had not seen any other Americans on our train. American tourists had not yet begun coming to Mexico. We were told that the Americans who were taken off the train and shot were engineers. Since the Revolution was over, I suspected we were told this story as a prank. But it gave us pause, nevertheless.

Here we were in this beautiful old colonial city for the first time. I was overwhelmed by everything I was seeing and hearing on all sides, and it was impossible for me to understand that Lowelito and I might not be liked at all by the Mexicans.

In any case I was determined to stay. My fascination for the life I was seeing in the streets of Guadalajara far outweighed any significance that shocking train incident might have had for us. We accepted the pleading of a hotel representative who had met the train, and let him take us, along with our baggage, to the Hotel Jardín, which seemed to be located right in the middle of things.

For a few days after our arrival I felt a little uneasy as I walked about with my paint box, easel, and stool, looking for subjects to paint. I tried to find places where there were no people around. Perhaps that is why I started painting in an old abandoned Spanish cemetery. It was completely deserted except for a family of Indians that had taken up residence in some of the crypts, which the family had cleared out and made into a fairly large room. But those Indians didn't pay any attention to me. That old cemetery was a beautiful, solitary, and quiet place. Orange trees loaded with fruit were growing among the graves and tombstones. People didn't seem to want to pick the oranges, perhaps, I imagined, because they were growing up out of the graves. I picked some, took them to our hotel, and tried them out on Lowelito. I did not tell him where I got the oranges, but noticed that he really liked them.

But as wonderful as we both found Guadalajara to be in the year 1923, we remained there only one month before making what turned out to be a most important move for us. It was also an unforeseen move, since I was completely happy in Guadalajara. Lowelito had come back to the hotel one afternoon filled with excitement.

"I've just met an old tramp, an American, in the plaza," he said, "and he told me of a wonderful lake, sixty miles long, just thirty or forty miles from here. He said there are little villages all around the lake, and that one of them, called Chapala, is fabulous. He said the lake also is called Chapala."

Lowelito was so enthusiastic about what he had learned from the tramp that I decided we had better get to that village of Chapala as soon as we could. And that is how it happened that we settled there.

In those days a little train ran down to Chapala from Guadalajara, but only twice a week, so the very next morning we were on it. We did not take our belongings—our paints, canvases, and so on—on that trip. We decided we had better see the place first. What we found was far beyond anything we could have imagined. Chapala in 1923 was not at all the way it is today, and even now it is a beautiful place. It was then more like some sort of overlooked paradise. Lowelito and I were speechless at what we had found.

We walked from the railroad depot, which was on the edge of the great silvery lake, down into the village with its red-tile-roofed houses. All the little houses that lined the streets were painted in pale pastel colors, and most of the men we met in the streets were dressed in white and had red sashes around their waists and wide-brimmed hats on their heads. The women all wore shawls, or rebozos, over their heads and shoulders. Soon we came to the central plaza, which had a little blue bandstand in the middle. Walking east from the plaza, we found, in the very first block, a house for rent. A boy on a bicycle told us that it had just been vacated. He said an English writer had been living there, and had only recently moved away. I did not learn until at least a year later that the English writer was D. H. Lawrence.

The people next door to this house gave us the name and address of the agent in Guadalajara from whom we could rent the house. We hurried back to the

railroad station and caught the little train back to the city. Before we retired that night in the Hotel Jardín, we had rented our house in Chapala.

*   *   *

The people who lived next door, toward the plaza, were the Pérez Arces. They were most helpful and friendly. Mrs. Pérez Arce fascinated me especially because she smoked cigarettes. At that time, few women back in the States smoked. But the way Señora Arce smoked showed that smoking was not a daring practice she had just recently taken up. You could tell that she smoked because her mother before her had smoked, as well as her grandmother. Señora Arce had a sister visiting her from Guadalajara who was very pretty. Señor Pérez Arce was an impressive gentleman about fifty years old. I did not fail to notice that whenever he went out on the street he wore a pistol at his waist. He spoke a little English, but didn't seem to like to. So I had to do the talking with him. Lowelito, at that time, didn't know one word of Spanish.

When we moved into our house that first day and looked the place over, we found that there was no stove in the kitchen. Instead of a stove, there was a cement shelf where a charcoal fire was supposed to be built. I had already bought some meat that morning for our supper. I had seen it hanging in an open meat market near the plaza. People were busy buying meat there even though it was so covered with flies you could barely see it. I had hesitated to buy it, but decided that if the people of Chapala didn't mind the flies then maybe I shouldn't be so squeamish. But in any case I intended to cook the meat well done, just to be on the safe side. Now I saw that I would have to light a charcoal fire on that shelf in the kitchen.

Lowelito and I had already been camping and baching together long enough to have worked out a pattern. It turned out that I had become the cook, while he had become the dishwasher and general handyman. So now I said to Lowelito, "We've got to have some charcoal. You run up to the market and get some. Take that basket, and when you find the charcoal in the marketplace just point at it and say, '*carbón.*' Say it with the accent on the last syllable. That's what they call charcoal down here." I suppose that was the first word in Spanish Lowelito learned.

Lowelito took the basket and went on his errand. As

Jesus Carillo,
"su servidor.
para servirle"

soon as he had gone, a little Mexican boy came walking into our patio, which was in the center of our house. He said that his name was Jesús and that he would like to have the job of "*regando la calle.*" I asked him what that meant.

"Every house in Chapala," he explained, "has to throw water in the street every morning, every day, including Sundays." He said that the *presidente municipal* (the mayor) demanded that every house water the street out in front every day. So I gave Jesús that job. He also told me that his mother would like to clean our house once a week, and I told him to tell her we would like that. Jesús said that his last name was Carrillo, that he was "*Jesús Carrillo, su servidor para servirle.*" I looked up the word *carrillo* in our English-Spanish dictionary and found that it meant "well pulley," which I thought was a good name for a boy whose job was to throw water into the street.

When Lowelito returned, he not only had a basket full of black, irregularly shaped charcoal, but also two cans of condensed milk and a box of Post Toasties.

"What are you going to do with that stuff?" I asked him. "We are not in the States now, you know. We are way down below the Tropic of Cancer, and you go buying stuff that is pure American." I also told him that we were going to have beefsteak for supper.

So I took the charcoal and made a neat pile of it on the cement shelf. Then I asked Lowelito to give me some matches. I began to light the matches and hold them to the charcoal, but the charcoal wouldn't light. Little Jesús stood watching me, and after I had used up a box of those Mexican matches, he said that next day he would bring me some *ocote* for building the fire. He seemed to think that tomorrow was soon enough for a fire.

We didn't get a charcoal fire lit that night, and ended up eating the Post Toasties and condensed milk for our first supper in our new home.

*   *   *

When Jesús Well-Pulley arrived early the next morning, he had with him a little bundle of *ocote*, which turned out to be fat pine. He placed a couple of the sticks on our stove-shelf, piled some charcoal over the sticks, and then stuck a match to the sticks. They flamed up brightly. After a moment or two, he began to fan the flame with a straw fan he had brought along. In a short time, we had a hot, glowing charcoal fire. I then sent Jesús for some eggs, bread, and coffee, and we had a good breakfast—without Post Toasties.

After we had sorted out our paints and other art materials, Lowelito started to work making a sign for our front door. Actually what he made, using red, gold, and black—was a kind of family crest. Underneath the crest, he made illuminated letters that read: "THE HOUSE WITH THE GREEN DOOR." Since our entrance door was the color of old unpainted wood—a dark gray color—I asked Lowelito just why he was naming our house "The House with the Green Door"?

"Because that is what it is," he told me. "Go look out the back."

I went through the kitchen and outside into a small garden area back there. The mountain called San Miguel, covered with tall trees, rose steeply from that place. When I turned around to go back into the house,

I found that we did indeed have a house with a green door. Nobody would ever see it, but it was there anyway, a bright-green back door. Since Lowelito's sign was written in English, I imagined that it would not puzzle the natives, who spoke and read only Spanish.

* * *

We were both eager to get to work. We had come to Chapala to draw and paint what we saw, and what we were seeing around us was a visual world of magic: bright sunshine and blue shadows up and down the streets, red tile roofs and roofs made of yellow thatch, banana trees waving above the red tile roofs, bougainvillaea of brilliant color hanging over old walls, the gray expanse of the lake, and a sky in which floated mountainous clouds. Finally, there were the beautiful people, in clothes of all colors—beautiful, happy, smiling, friendly people—and donkeys, horses, cows, hogs, and dogs of all sizes, colors, and shapes.

Lowelito liked to draw with a pencil. He must have been a close observer, for I noticed that he could make drawings of the natives without having them pose for him. I don't suppose he could make a true portrait of an individual that way, but either the drawings he began to turn out looked like the people we were seeing around us every day, or else, after looking at his drawings, I would start seeing the people the way he had seen them.

I preferred to paint with oil colors on canvas, my favorite subject matter being the houses the people lived in, especially the straw-thatched houses of the Indians. These were found outside the village, away from the streets. Some were located right on the water's edge, and because the lake rose at times, these houses were often built on stilts. The people who lived in the straw houses at the edge of the lake were fishermen, who used nets to catch small fish called *charales*. These little white fish were spread out on the ground or on the roofs of the houses to dry in the sun. When very dry, they could be eaten like potato chips. Often I would be offered this food when I was painting near a fisherman's house. At first, I would accept the kind offer only to be polite, but before long I developed a taste for the dried *charales*.

The people who lived in the straw houses away from the lake were mostly farmers, who raised crops like corn, beans, and squash. Always there were clumps of castor-bean plants next to their houses. I was told that this plant was poisonous, but I found that it was pretty when seen with the houses.

When I recall how I went about painting pictures of those Indian houses, I begin to wonder about the value of knowledge for a painter. In those days, I was completely innocent of art theories and had no knowledge about how a picture should be made. But I do know how careful I was to choose the viewpoint from which to see my subject. In fact, there were times when a group of houses would not look right to me wherever I stood. I seemed to know exactly where I should place my easel and stool, even though I could never have explained why. I seemed to have had something built into me that guided my choice. And once my easel was in position, I am sure I painted the houses exactly the way I saw them and not the way I thought about them. In fact, when I looked at the houses with the intention of painting them, they were not even houses. They were only colored shapes, and all the colored shapes together formed one big embracing shape. That is really what I saw. But there was something else included, for when I looked at the houses and saw them as one group I also noticed that they had a happy expression.

One morning, very early, I had walked quite a distance looking for a subject to paint. As I passed some little straw houses that did not seem to be paintable, I was nevertheless pleased by the sound of women patting out tortillas inside. My paint box, easel, and stool were so heavy that my left arm had become cramped. I knew I would have to rest it before I could handle my paintbrushes. I stopped, put down my things, and sat on a rock against a cliff, which was on the far side of the mountain San Miguel. I was waiting until the blood got back into my painting arm. I then walked up a nearby hill, and when I reached its crest, there before me in a little draw was a whole community of beautiful straw houses. They were held together, visually, in a delightful, compact group. It was clear to me that I was in the right spot from which to see and paint the subject. I put up my folding easel, attached my canvas to it so the wind would not blow it off, and began to paint what I was seeing. My painting and my seeing became one and the same activity, while the group of houses seemed to be taking part in the process.

The painting was nearly completed in a short time, but I noticed a certain area on my canvas that called for the shape of a woman. So, with my paints, I put her there—in a red blouse. When I looked up at that same spot among the houses, to my astonishment there stood that woman in the same red blouse. She had not been there before, but I had painted her exactly as she appeared, nevertheless. I felt I had somehow created that

woman, and I also had the feeling that I should gather up my materials and leave that place immediately.

*   *   *

I had walked three or four miles before finding that group of straw houses I had painted, and now as I approached the village, carrying my heavy equipment, my arm had become quite paralyzed again. The handle on my painting box had given way, causing me to have to carry the box under my arm in a cramped position.

Looking ahead toward the village, I saw Lowelito approaching with his drawing pad. He was wearing a light-brown sweater and high laced-up boots, his usual attire. Walking along with him was a small man in white *calzones* (trousers) with a red sash around his waist. This person suddenly started running toward me, leaving Lowelito behind. When he came up close, I saw that he was only a boy, about twelve or thirteen years old. He immediately took my paint box and easel from me. Apparently he had seen that I was struggling with a heavy load.

"I am Isidoro," he said. "I shall carry your things to your house."

Although he was dressed like the Indians and was wearing *guaraches* (native sandals), he looked more like a mestizo. He kept a broad smile on his face continuously.

"I would like to carry your equipment for you all the time," he said. "My name is Isidoro Pulido, and I do not have a house of my own."

"All right, Isidoro," I told him. "I go out every day, and you can come along and help me carry my equipment."

That is how I met Isidoro, who would prove to be my faithful friend for many years thereafter.

*   *   *

The word *pulido* means "polished" or "nice," so now we had added to our household Jesús Well-Pulley and Isidoro Nice. Isidoro had told me that he did not have a house of his own, so I was not surprised when he turned up that night and slept on the floor just inside the entrance to our house. The floor was hard cement in the entrance way, with little pebbles scattered about in the cement. I told Lowelito that we had better get a bed for Isidoro and let him sleep in the kitchen. But when I suggested that to Isidoro he laughed and said he preferred to sleep on the floor, and that he wanted to sleep in the entrance way in order to guard our house. At night, he would wrap himself in his heavy bright red *cobija* (blanket) and apparently sleep soundly on that hard floor. During the daytime, he would carry the blanket folded and hung over his left shoulder. I had noticed that all the Indians did that, except that their *cobijas* were usually a dark rich gray with bright-colored flowers around the slit for the neck. The Indians would often stick their heads through that slit, wearing the *cobija* as a poncho.

Lowelito still only knew one Spanish word, *carbón*, which he had learned when he went after charcoal, but I felt sure he would begin to pick up the Spanish language with Isidoro around.

One morning, Lowelito told me that Isidoro wanted to make a vegetable garden in that little space outside the green door. I knew Lowelito was beginning to learn Spanish or he would not have understood what Isidoro wanted to do. I thought it was a good idea to have vegetables growing back there, so I asked Isidoro what he needed for that project.

"Only seed," he said. "I have a friend who owns two fine burros, and I can get all the burro manure I need for the garden."

He told me that burro manure was "*muy rico*" (very rich), and that it would make even asparagus grow fast. The very next day he went for the burro manure. I watched him prepare the earth back there for the vegetables. He worked furiously, digging up the dirt and mixing it with the manure. Finally he had a large bed of earth, raised about eight inches higher than the surrounding space. Although Isidoro's garden was only about eight by ten feet in size, it was not long before we were getting a good supply of vegetables from it.

We did not have a cook. The mother of Jesús Well-Pulley came every Tuesday morning to clean our house, but I did the cooking. The mother of Jesús also threw water. She did not throw it into the street like her son—she threw it all over our house. When she arrived to clean, Lowelito and I knew we had better clear out at once, for she immediately began to throw water around. She did not seem to need a broom. Her idea of cleaning our house was to flush everything out into the street. Her son was supposed to take over from there. Fortunately all our floors were either cement or tile, and they would dry shortly after she departed with her buckets and rags.

Although I was the cook, we would often go at noon to a little restaurant up the street, beyond the plaza. It was at that restaurant that we met a young Mexican by the name of Alberto Garay Enríquez, who was the baggage man on the little train that ran to and from Guadalajara twice a week. Lowelito and I would try to go to the restaurant on those days when Alberto would be there. In the restaurant, all three of us would invariably order *pescado blanco* (white fish) for lunch, and it would always arrive on our plates with the head intact. The fish was a real delicacy, but neither Lowelito nor I could stand the looks of the fish head with its eye staring at us. We never touched the fish head. When Alberto noticed this neglect, he asked if he might have our fish heads. "The head is the best part of the fish," he would say, "because of its eyes." And he would gouge out the eyes and eat them, smacking his lips and rolling his eyes as though nothing tasted so delicious. After lunch, we would stroll down the street together toward the lake, past the Mólgora Hotel. Whenever a pretty girl would come along,

Alberto would say the only words in English he seemed to have learned. "Good for one night," he would say.

It seemed obvious to us that Chapala was made up of two distinct parts, only one of which seemed to us to deserve our attention. Certainly we would never have dreamed of making drawings or paintings of one of those parts, while the other was a constant inspiration. Along the lake below the Mólgora Hotel was part one, a long string of elegant and very large houses, most of which were in a sad state of neglect. Extending out from some of those houses on the lakeshore were piers, and they also were battered and broken. Quite obviously these houses had flourished before the Mexican Revolution, and had belonged to wealthy people. The last house of this group down the lakeshore was El Manglar, which we were told had once been the summer home of President Porfirio Díaz, the old Mexican dictator who had been thrown out by the revolution. Unlike the other houses of this group, this one had a Spanish flavor. And it was backed up by a dark grove of mango trees, which gave the house its name.

The other part of Chapala, the truly beautiful part to us, was composed of the red-tile-roofed houses in which the poor people lived and those straw houses farther out of town.

It had not taken us long to discover that there were also two distinct classes of people in Chapala. There were the Indian people and there were those Lowelito called "the *elegante*." Perhaps it could be said that there were the poor and the rich, but those terms would not really tell the true story about the people of Chapala at that time. One might have expected to find the rich living in those impressive old houses along the lakeshore, but most of those old houses were abandoned, completely neglected from the looks of them. In one of them, however, there did live a Russian woman and a man who was said to be her brother. In the late afternoons, just before dark, thousands of leather-wing bats would start going into the upper part of that large house. Watching those bats going in to roost, I always hoped that the Russians lived on the lowest floor, away from the bats.

I now believe that the difference between the two classes of people in Chapala was basically a matter of attitude, a matter of life-style, and a matter of ego development. Lowelito and I were very respectful of the Indian people. We felt that they were in touch with something eternal. It was as though they identified themselves with the past and the future, but not so much with the present. The *elegante*, on the other hand, were people of the present. They thought about what was going on in the world. They were "modern." The Indians were not like that. The latest world news did not even reach them. I once said to Lowelito that the Indians of Chapala reminded me of what I had read about the Bedouins of the Sinai Peninsula, who keep on going their own way through time, despite all the change taking place around them. Lowelito and I had an almost humble respect and admiration for those Indian people. We did not dislike the others, but we felt that we had come to Mexico only to visit the Indians.

*   *   *

As one stood facing the entrance to our house, the house of the Pérez Arce family joined ours on the right, while on the left lived a family that remained quite un-

known to us, but not unnoticed. In that house that joined
ours on the left lived a señorita who was for me a beautiful Spanish type. She had black hair, big brown eyes,
long eyelashes, a fair complexion, and a seductive figure. But despite her beauty, Lowelito always referred to
her as "the Chinless Wonder." I was inclined to resent
that name he had given her, for after I heard it I found
myself looking at her chin whenever I saw her, instead
of appreciating her overall beauty. But despite her re-
ceding chin a young doctor, who had a corner drugstore
on the plaza, fell in love with her. For several weeks
thereafter, we did not get our sleep out. The doctor had
hired an orchestra to play and sing under her window
every morning before daylight. Our window was close
to hers, so we also got that daily love serenade. But finally it stopped, and the two were married. Lowelito
said she had to marry the doctor or die of insomnia.

*   *   *

The woman who came each Tuesday morning to
wash the floors of our house could never have been ac-
cused of winning a beauty contest, but when it came to
dashing buckets of water and flooding floors she was a
pro. Her tools for cleaning our house were a couple of
buckets, a long-handled mop, and some rags. She did
not use a broom.

Her little son, Jesús, who threw water into the street
every day, looked very much like his mother. They both
had small pug noses. Jesús had a cowlick over the back
of his head, which made his hair stand on end behind.
Since his mother never removed her rebozo, regardless

of how hard she worked, I could not tell whether or not she had such a cowlick herself. But I assumed that since their noses were exactly alike, she also had that cowlick. When Jesús applied for the job of watering the street, I liked his serious, businesslike manner, but thought I had never seen an uglier face. In fact, I was so intrigued by his face that I wanted to make a drawing of it. If anything, the mother was even less attractive than the son, possibly because she was feminine.

"If a person is going to look ugly," Lowelito said, "that person should be a man and not a woman."

"How do you figure that?" I asked Lowelito.

"Because a woman who is ugly is a disapointment," he said, "and an ugly man is not a disappointment. You couldn't care less that he is ugly. But," he continued, "women like ugly men better than pretty ones."

I said that that depended on what he meant by a "pretty" man.

One Tuesday morning, Señora Carrillo arrived earlier than usual, but Lowelito and I were ready for her. We had placed all the things we didn't want to get wet on top of a table, and we were ready to evacuate the house until she had finished her work. But this time Señora Carrillo arrived with another person. Instead of leaving the house when she entered with her equipment, as we usually did, in order to give her complete freedom with her buckets of water, we followed her back into our patio. We did this because we were so surprised and stunned by the beauty of the girl who had swept past us with our cleaning woman that we wanted to find out more about her. Lowelito was so affected by the looks of the girl that he overtook Señora Carrillo and assisted her with her buckets. If I was less hypnotized, it was because I had recently met a girl in San Diego, California, who had partly blinded me to all other girls.

Señora Carrillo was now beaming, for she well knew the reason we had not gone on out into the street. So, putting down her buckets and smiling broadly, she now said, "I want to present to you *mi hijita* (my little daughter), Alicia."

Lowelito immediately began talking to Alicia—in English. I knew the beautiful girl could not understand English, but clearly that did not matter. That was all Lowelito had for talking, and the way the two of them were looking at each other, while he was talking English and she saying words in Spanish, made it obvious that they were communicating without difficulty. She never looked at me once. She had not noticed that I was present. So I left the field to him, picked up my paint box and easel from the kitchen table, and went out of the house. I had the thought that our floors would not be clean and dry for hours, and that I might as well spend the rest of the day out painting. I was also wondering why it was that all girls liked Lowelito so much. To me he did not have a very ugly face, which, according to him, a man needed if he wanted girls to like him.

Isidoro was not around at the time, so I carried my painting equipment without his help. The street that went by our house was called Calle Hidalgo. It went right through the village and on to Ajijic, some six miles away. About two blocks down this street there was a stretch that was always in deep shadow because of the big trees that bordered it on the right. On the lake side along that stretch was a beautiful old stone wall with some bright-purple bougainvillaea hanging over it in several places. Behind that wall and down toward the lake was that old house in which lived the Russians and, at night, all those leather-wing bats. That stretch of road, which was unpaved, was also a favorite place for hogs during the warm part of the day. The hogs would sleep in the shadows. It always amused me the way they would complain when any sunshine would break through and destroy the shadows they were sleeping in. When that happened, the hogs would grunt and move over to other shadows. They were obviously annoyed at who-ever it was that had the nerve to move their shadows.

I set up my easel at one end of that stretch of road because the place was for me mysterious and magical. Although only a place, it seemed to have a real person-ality. I decided to paint it as a street scene and include all the hogs sleeping in the shadows. I went to work trying to put it all on my canvas. I wanted to show the road as moving slowly through all the dark shadow shapes and sunlight shapes, with the lazy hogs asleep in the shad-ows. The old stone wall would be on the left side and the tall trees would be marching along on the right. For a while, I was lost in what I was doing, but suddenly, to my surprise, all the hogs began to shuffle to their feet and move off the road to the right, grunting ferociously. Then I heard a sound like thunder behind me. But it was not thunder. It was that Russian woman riding at full gallop on a dark horse, and she was coming right at me. Fortunately, she made her horse swerve just as she reached my position. She knocked my easel over but missed me. By then all the hogs were safely up the hill-side, among the trees. She never slowed down, but kept galloping at full speed down the road.

I went back to my work, and when I thought my

painting was completed I gathered up my equipment
and started home. Only a short distance from where I
had been painting the street scene, I came to where
there was a small open field on the lake side of the street.
I had not noticed that place while walking in the opposite direction. Scattered over the field were dry yellow
cornstalks left over from the harvest of the year before.
On the border of this field, leading down toward the
lake from the street, was a low stone wall, and rising
from behind that wall was a long row of immense eu-
calyptus trees. They literally shot up like fireworks into
the space above. I was shocked by what I was seeing.
The bright afternoon sunlight was striking the tall trees,
turning the whole area into a blaze of vibrating color
and movement. All the space in front of the trees seemed
to be charged with some kind of energy. To me it was a
revelation. I felt as though I had surprised among those
trees a living spirit, and that it was staring down at me. I
knew I would have to set up my easel there and try to
paint what I had seen. My only worry was that it might
not be there, at least as I had seen it, when I returned.

When I got back to the House with the Green Door,
I discovered that the cleaning woman was gone, and so
were Lowelito and the beautiful girl. I placed my painting of the street scene against a wall in the open patio
and began to study it. What I found was that the shadows I had painted looked like dark, heavy rugs spread
over the road, with hogs sleeping on them. I knew that I
had yet to learn how to make shapes look like shadows
and not like black rugs. I would have to paint that magical place again, despite the danger of that wild-riding
Russian horsewoman.

*   *   *

Lowelito must have returned late that night, for after I went to bed I did not hear him come in. The thought that he might be singing a love song under Alicia's barred window amused me and helped put me to sleep.

The next morning, Lowelito was up ahead of me. He had built a charcoal fire with *ocote* and had put a pot of coffee on it by the time I arrived in the kitchen. As I started wondering what we would have for breakfast, someone began knocking on our entrance door. When I opened the big heavy door, I saw an old woman standing before me. She was wrapped in a dark *rebozo*. The bone structure of her brown leathery face was emphasized by the way her iron-gray hair was stretched tightly down around it. She held out to me her bony hands, in which she had two white eggs.

"*Compra estos blanquillos,*" she said.

I bought them from the old lady, which solved my problem of breakfast.

The moment breakfast was over, I began getting my painting materials together, for I could think of nothing but those tall trees down Calle Hidalgo. There was no need to hurry, however, for I would have to wait until the sun would be in the right place to throw its light upon the trees.

While I was waiting for the sun to move into the right position, Isidoro showed up. He picked up my paint box and my easel and stool, so that I carried only my canvas. We then went down to the spot where I wanted to paint. I was glad that Isidoro did not stay with

me. I wanted to give my undivided attention to what I
hoped to do.

The sun was in the right place. But would that
strange effect be there again? I waited with my eyes
open and tried to think of nothing at all. I then raised
my eyes and focused them some distance beyond the tall
trees and the old stone wall. Suddenly the subject came
alive again, as it had done the day before. There it was.
That spirit was again back among the foliage and the
tree trunks. It was invisible, but it was nevertheless present, and it was looking at me. I began to paint as though
I myself had nothing to do with my painting activity.
Did that spirit in the trees have hold of my arm, causing
my brushes to take up colors from my palette and apply
them to the canvas? I felt as though my painting were
being done for me. My canvas became covered with
many colors, and I knew that energy, movement, and
light were also involved. Eventually there was nothing
more to do. It was as though an electric switch had been
turned off. The process, whatever it was, had run its
course.

I cleaned my smeared palette, folded my easel, and
closed my paint box. I then carried these things and the
canvas up the street and back to the House with the
Green Door. As before, I placed my painting against the
patio wall, where I could study it in a good light. What I
saw was completely meaningless: no wall, no trees, no
spirit, no energy. The result of my activity was obviously
a complete failure.

Every time I would pass that place thereafter, I
would look at it, and it would look at me. I thought I
could hear it saying, "You can't paint me! You waste
your time trying to paint me!" There developed be-

tween us a genuine, almost friendly relationship, but I never tried to paint that wonderful place again.

If I had been painting solely under the influence of inspiration that day, I now knew that something else had to be added if a good painting was to be created.

*   *   *

When Lowelito and I first arrived in Chapala, we did not see any other Americans. The two Russians who lived in the house with the bats were the only other non-Mexicans in the village, as far as we knew. And during the next year and a half, while we were living in the House with the Green Door, no other Americans showed up. I think the Mexican Revolution, which had gone on so long and with such ferocity, had done a good job of frightening American tourists. But a short distance beyond our house, in the direction of Ajijic, there was a street with the name "Calle de Mister Crow" (Street of Mr. Crow). I was never able to learn who Mr. Crow was or why the street was named for him, but I assumed that he was an American, and I considered it a compliment that the Mexicans of Chapala had named a street after an American.

We lost all track of time. We were so busy painting and drawing one might have believed we were being paid to do it. Every morning we would go out. We would return around noon and then go out again in the afternoon. About the only other thing I did during that time was write letters to that black-haired girl I had met in California, and even those letters were illustrated by drawings of Chapala. Isidoro would help me carry my equipment. Sometimes we would walk a long distance

before I would find a subject that appealed to me. But after I had my easel up and anchored with rocks against the wind, Isidoro would go back to see if Lowelito had anything for him to do. Lowelito did not need him to help with his equipment, since he only used pencils and a small drawing pad.

This routine went on for over a year before we thought of visiting any of the villages around the lake. Then one day Lowelito came in and informed me that he had hired a boat with an outboard motor to carry us up the lake to a village called Muscala. Later I learned that the village was called *Mes*cala, not Muscala, as Isidoro pronounced it. Isidoro told us it was dangerous to go to Mescala because the people living there didn't like foreigners at all.

Taking along a lunch, we climbed into the little

canoe and started up the sixty-five-mile-long lake. In those days, there was no road leading to Mescala, only a foot trail. The easiest way to go was by boat. With the outboard motor, it took us several hours to reach the place. Having once arrived on the lakeshore out in front of the village, we then had to climb over a seemingly endless number of rock fences, which formed a complex barricade of small fields between the lakeshore and the village. Approaching Mescala over those rock fences, I was reminded of Gauguin's South Sea Island paintings. The scene was composed of clearly divided units: gray rock fences forming outlines around fields of green, these in turn seen against light brown adobe houses with red tile roofs, and above all this a rolling dark green mass of mango trees. Once we reached the streets, we found that they were paved with gray cobblestones. The houses along both sides of each street formed solid walls with closed doorways and were made of dark yellow-ochre adobe from which most of the outer covering of plaster had fallen away. The whole village seemed to be a part of the earth upon which it stood.

When we reached Mescala that day, after climbing over all the rock fences, the place appeared to be completely deserted. No one was in sight. We walked to the plaza and looked at the stark old church there. Strung out on wires above the front yard of the church were hundreds of little cut paper decorations, which must have been left over from a recent fiesta. We strolled all over the village, hoping that someone eventually would come out of one of the houses, but no one emerged. I asked Isidoro if the streets were deserted because this was the siesta hour.

"No," he said, "the people are in their houses because we are in their streets. When we leave, they will
come out."

Mescala was certainly a beautiful place to paint.
The dark mango trees rising above the red-tile-roofed
houses, the light-grean banana trees peeping over old
walls, the bright purple bougainvillaea, the red-orange
color of the earth, and especially the silence of the place,
made me wish that Mescala were nearer Chapala so that I
could paint there often. But the strange behavior of the
people—their staying out of sight—caused me to wonder about Isidoro's belief that the place was dangerous.

The sun was getting low, and already the sky was a
blazing deep red when we got into our little boat and
started back to Chapala.

But we could not get Mescala off our minds. We
had not been back in Chapala more than a week when
Lowelito made the bold suggestion that we go to Mescala and live there for a month or two. When Isidoro
learned of that plan, he said again that we would be taking our lives in our hands. We decided to go back to see
if it were possible to rent a house in the village. Lowelito
pointed out that we could keep the House with the Green
door, just close it up for a month or so and then return
to it.

Two days after making that decision we set out early
in the morning to go by the foot trail. Isidoro went
along with us, for he knew the trail well. On the way up
from Chapala, after walking several hours, we stopped
at a small *ranchería* near the shore, where we had lunch
with a family of Indians who were friends of Isidoro's. I
shall never forget their friendly hospitality, nor the delicious lunch they served us under the thatched roof of a

dirt-floored *ramada* (a room with a back wall but open on the front and sides). Whatever it is that causes the Indians in this area to make their primitive houses and utensils so charming and artistic must also be what causes them to make their simple food so delicious. It may be that this unique talent is, to some extent, at least, a carry-over from pre-Spanish times. Corn tortillas and beans, which were the staple diet before the Spaniards arrived, were served us that day. Our hostess mashed the beans into a paste and fried them on a flat ceramic frying pan, but she heated the tortillas by throwing them directly onto a bed of glowing charcoal. In addition, we were served chicken in a red chili sauce, which may also have been an ancient dish, except that in pre-Columbian times wild duck or domesticated turkey would probably have taken the place of chicken. This area of Mexico, unlike the Central Plateau, was never overpopulated; therefore there was no depletion of wild game. So we felt certain, as we enjoyed the delicious lunch, that the ancestors of these people would never have served us a dish of human flesh, as the Aztecs might have done. In this western area human sacrifice was practiced on a small scale, and never, as has been said of the Aztecs, to provide protein to the daily diet. We invited these friends of Isidoro's to visit us sometime whenever they were in Chapala. They accepted our invitation with sincere thanks and eventually visited us there.

When we arrived in Mescala this time, we went into the streets, and, just as before, nobody was in sight. So we continued on to the plaza. Isidoro began to scout around. He went over to a house, and from where we were standing we saw that he had found someone and was talking through an open window, Isidoro was telling this person that the two North Americans with him wanted to come and live in Mescala.

The streets of Mescala never filled with people that day, but from different directions the city fathers began to assemble, arriving one at a time and going into a building just off the plaza. Lowelito and I also entered this building, for we wanted to express in person our wish to come live in Mescala if no one had any objections and if there was a house to rent. The reason we gave was that we were artists and wanted to paint pictures of Mescala, which we considered a most beautiful place.

These city fathers—all picturesque old Indians— went into a discussion, and we were told that if we would remain seated on a bench in an adjoining room, a decision would be given us later. I was now reminded of a similar occasion, several years before, when Lowelito and I had asked to be allowed to camp on a Kickapoo Indian reservation in the far northern Mexico state of Coahuila. Those Kickapoo Indian city fathers in their village at the head of the Sabinas River had come together in much the same way as these Indians of Mescala. The decision they had reached was that we could not camp on their reservation. Apparently they did not like the idea of a couple of white Americans pitching a tent right in the middle of their own straw houses. They did, however, send one of their tribesmen with us to show us a good campsite some eight miles down the river in a pretty pecan grove.

Here, about thirteen hundred miles farther south, it interested us to see these old Mescalan men discussing our request in the same way. Remembering that earlier affair with the Kickapoo village council, we were surprised when we were told that we could come and live in Mescala. The Mescalans' willingness to let us live in their village, while the Kickapoos had refused us, probably was a small indication that the Mescalans were no longer as "Indian" as the Kickapoos.

One of the Mescalan councilmen was now delegated to go and show us where we might live, just as the Kickapoos had sent one of their own men to show us where we might camp off their limits. Here in Mescala, however, we were permitted not only to live in the village, but also to choose just about whatever house we wished to occupy.

Our guide, a councilman, took us right into the inner family circles of those Mescalan houses and showed the houses to us without bothering to explain to the residents what it was all about. Finally, I mentioned to the guide that all the houses he was showing us seemed to be in use, since there were so many people and dogs and chickens in them. To this he replied that the occupants of the one we wanted could move. Such hospitality on his part was in sharp contrast to the looks the occupants themselves were giving us as we walked about through their dining rooms and kitchens. It was also in contrast to the way the Mescalans were prone to go inside their houses and remain out of sight while we were in their streets. Because of all this Isidoro kept saying that one day the people of Mescala were going to throw all the rocks in their fences at us.

In the end, Lowelito and I did not go and live in Mescala. In the course of my conversations with our guide, I learned that the mail never was delivered to Mescala. There was no sign of a post office there, and if anyone wanted mail he would have to go himself to some

other place to get it. I could not stand the thought that I
would be completely out of touch with that girl I had
met in California. She wrote to me almost daily, often
enclosing in her letters clippings from newspapers, and
I had come to depend upon her letters. If a person can
fall in love by mail, that seemed to be happening to me.

*   *   *

We put the idea of living in Mescala out of our
minds, and went back to our routine of painting and
drawing as though there had been no distraction. I began to have a good feeling that I was putting down on
my canvas precisely what I was seeing, and also how I
was seeing it. I came to the conclusion that that was what
a painter should do, even if he starved to death in the
process. But that pleasant period of work without distraction was not to last. The Devil himself must have noticed the progress we were making and figured out a
way to foul up our work.

In addition to making beautiful drawings—of the
Chapala people, views of the lake, street scenes, and so
on—Lowelito was also learning to speak Spanish. He
was certainly not learning it from a book. It seemed to
me that he was acquiring Spanish the same way one's
clothes get soiled: without conscious effort. He was just
"picking it up" from talking with the Indians, and as a
result he was becoming like Isidoro—speaking a language, while at the same time remaining illiterate in it.
Neither he nor Idisoro could read Spanish or write it.
The way Lowelito was learning Spanish was harmonious
with the way he lived. He moved along the lines of least
resistance. Whenever an obstacle would turn up in his

pathway, he would not bother to remove it—he would
go around it. If too many obstacles confronted him he
would go to some other place, when there were none.

In the summer of 1925 there arrived in Chapala an
American who announced that he was a student of

philosophy. I think he said he *was* a philosopher. From the very first day he arrived, Lowelito ceased to learn Spanish.

That philosopher who came to Chapala meant well, but Lowelito and I did not know how to deal with him. He wore native Indian clothes, although everything else about his physical appearance was non-Indian. He had very white skin, reddish hair, and blue eyes, and he was tall and heavy. Yet the clothes he wore were Indian right down to the sandals with a thong between his toes. And, as though desirous of creating as un-Indian an effect as possible while wearing Indian clothes, he was at all times noisy.

This philosopher first approached us as a fellow American. Thereafter, in the same way, he came each morning to our house to sit and talk, to shout and dance by himself, and to extend invitations to go and have beer or lunch with him as his guests. His insistence was such that we did not know how to refuse, despite the fact that this new social life was interfering with what we wanted to do. He was no doubt socially mature, while we were socially maladjusted in those days. Suddenly it seemed to us that we were caught in a trap. We came to realize that he had extended his hospitality to us and it was now up to us to extend ours or else feel guilty. But in the meantime we would find ourselves drinking more of his beer and even dining at his house again, although we had not wanted to.

No sooner could we finish our breakfast than that philosopher would arrive at our house to sit and talk in our patio. What he talked about almost always seemed to be something we should have known about, but something we had never heard of or thought of before. We were always saying, "Oh, yes." We were always trying to hide our ignorance. We had not known how ignorant we were before he arrived in Chapala, and while we should have felt thankful toward him for revealing our ignorance to us, what we really felt was that there must be some place where we could go and forget our ignorance.

Lowelito already had insulted this new acquaintance by talking too loud about his faults one day when we were in the bathhouse across the street from our place. The Philosopher happened to be in the bathroom next to ours, and the walls were as thin as paper. After Lowelito had expressed what he felt about him in a loud voice, the Philosopher hollered through the thin walls to us to let us know he was present. But when we next saw him, neither he nor we mentioned that accidental incident.

One morning, we heard him coming loudly to our house before we had yet unlocked our front door. When he began pounding on the door, Lowelito motioned to me to keep quiet. "He will go away," said Lowelito in a whisper.

We stood there in our patio, holding still in our tracks and looking at the door, while the Philosopher stood in the street outside and beat on the door and called out our names.

"He will think we are not at home," Lowelito whispered, "and he will go away."

But instead, the Philosopher kept on pounding and calling until finally we could stand it no longer.

"Oh, is that you?" I said as I opened the door.

He came on in, smiling, and with him was our neighbor's dachshund dog, which, although our enemy, was now acting as though he was overjoyed to find us at home. He even raised his hind leg and pissed on the floor to show how at home he felt. Our other guest did not act at all overjoyed, but at least he did not embarrass us with questions. So Lowelito and I felt more obligated to him and his way of life than ever before. The next night, we left Chapala and went to Guanajuato. We did not tell the Philosopher we were leaving.

2
Guanajuato

There was no question in our minds about where we were going when we left Chapala. We were going to a place called Guanajuato. A young Mexican we had met, a graduate of Columbia University, who spoke fluent English, had told us that since we were art students we should not fail to visit Guanajuato. He did not describe Guanajuato to us, but the way he said we should see the place convinced us that we should go there.

Instead of going the short way, by bus, we decided to go by train and stop off in Mexico City. It was much easier to get my big steamer trunk to Guanajuato by train, for we could check it on the baggage car right on through. We wanted to go by way of the capital because we had heard rumors that the Mexican artists Diego Rivera and Orozco were painting murals there.

On the train in Mexico City, I could not help recalling what we had been told about those American engineers being shot on the train that preceded ours to Guadalajara. But during all our time in Chapala the Mexicans had been most friendly to us, and nothing unpleasant happened to us on this trip.

When we arrived in Mexico City, we knew we were only passing through on our way to Guanajuato, but it seemed important, especially to Lowelito, to stop over and see the Mexican murals. My own viewpoint at that time was close to being that of the Impressionists. I was becoming more aware of "images," and less and less concerned with what I knew about them. As a result, I was discovering in the world around me shapes and colors I had never seen before. Because of my own new way of seeing, I could not be very interested in how other artists were seeing. But I was glad to stop over anyway, since Lowelito was so eager to see the Mexican wall paintings.

Leaving the railroad station and walking in the direction of the Zócalo, we came to a house along the street with a sign in front that read, "*casa de huéspedes*" (boardinghouse), and we moved in. We then took a taxi and went to see some of the murals in public buildings. Lowelito found them very exciting, but my innocent impression was that they were like funny-paper drawings, only much more refined. At that time, my preoccupation with my own painting was blinding me to other viewpoints in art.

We returned to our boardinghouse. In this house there was an intimate dining room with small tables at which the people living there took their meals. We went down to breakfast the first morning and ordered *huevos rancheros*. When the eggs arrived, all covered with chili peppers and hot sauce, I watched with fascination as Lowelito reached over to a bottle filled with some sort of dark brown liquid and began shaking the liquid all over his eggs. Lowelito in those days was beginning to be in an experimental mood in his drawing, and apparently it was flowing over into his everyday living. I did not follow his example with the dark brown liquid, for it seemed to me that the eggs were already floating in strange liquids, in addition to having peppers, onions, and cheese scattered over them. After breakfast, we met a pleasant Mexican who had been sitting near us at one of the small tables. In the course of our talk with him he commented that Lowelito was the only man he had ever seen who poured coffee over his eggs. The dark brown liquid in the bottle was very strong coffee, which was supposed to be poured into a cup of hot water or hot milk.

After departing from Mexico City early the next morning, we came to a little town called Tula in the state of Hidalgo. It looked so pleasant to us from the train window that we got off there. All the way up to Tula that morning, we had looked at millions of spider webs stretched between the bushes parallel to the railroad track. The sun was shining on them, and because they were wet with dew they glistened like diamonds. Riding a hundred miles through those beautiful spider webs must have caused us to feel that Tula was our destination instead of Guanajuato. We spent the night in a hotel that was more like a jail than a hotel. Our room was like a prison cell, with four solid walls and not a single window in it. Tula turned out to be less interesting than we hoped Guanajuato would be. We did not know then, nor did archaeologists know, that Tula was the site of that ancient Toltec city called Tollán, which is mentioned in some of the ancient manuscripts of both the peoples of the Central Plateau and the Mayas of southeastern Mexico. We did, however, notice some monuments of stone in the vicinity, and also some broken stone figures in the walls of several buildings in

Tula. All of the monuments and figures seemed to us to be in the style of those at Teotihuacán.

After leaving Tula by train, we had to change to a smaller one at Silao to get to Guanajuato. We arrived in Guanajuato in the dead of night, in pitch darkness. It was so dark you couldn't see your hand in front of your face. It was one of those Mexican dark nights we had learned about in Chapala. I do not know what the hour of our arrival was, for in those days neither Lowelito nor I had a watch. We did not believe in owning a watch.

At the Guanajuato station, we found one cab drawn by one horse. Since we were the only passengers to get off the train, the driver of the cab was delighted when we asked him to take us to a hotel. We told him that we would like to have a good hotel, but *no de lujo* (not a luxurious one).

We got in the cab, and the driver set off into the black night. Because of the sound of the horse's hooves, we knew the street was of cobblestone. That was the only sound we could hear, and there were no lights anywhere. No dogs were barking and no church bells were ringing, which we later learned they did in Guanajuato on the hour. After we had been riding for about twenty minutes, and after the cab had made a number of ninety-degree turns from one street into another, we saw ahead of us a small electric light extended out into the street over a doorway in a stone wall. The electric light revealed a very narrow street between black walls.

The dark doorway opened directly into a small room, which was the hotel lobby. In a chair sat a Mexican man who was sound asleep with both feet on top of a desk in front of him. Lowelito didn't want to awaken him, but I said, "We've got to wake him if we want to stay here." So I knocked on the desk, and the Mexican came to. He turned out to be very pleasant. I was surprised at how awake he became almost immediately. We signed in and were guided up a stairway, very dimly lighted, to a room on the second floor at the rear of the hotel. In this room were two small beds, and at the back of the room, against the outside wall, was a small bathroom enclosed with walls that extended only about halfway up to the ceiling. Everything suited us fine, for we knew we would try later to find a place to rent that was similar to what we had had in Chapala. Here we were in a place called Guanajuato, where we could forget our ignorance, explore, and go on with our painting and drawing. We had no idea what Guanajuato would be like when we could see it in the daylight. We had read nothing about it.

The rest of that night, I must have slept very well, for I did not hear any church bells ring nor any dogs bark.

It was bright daylight when I awakened. Lying in bed, I was aware of a continuous buzzing and chattering sort of noise coming from the street, punctuated now and then by the sound of wheels going over cobblestones or by the cry of a vendor yelling to advertise something he had for sale. This overall sound was not like the one at Chapala. I realized then that every place—every village or town—has its own distinctive sound, which must be the auditory expression of its spirit. I got up and went into the bathroom, where there was a window in the outside wall. I wanted to know how the spirit of Guanajuato would look. I was completely unprepared for what I saw. I yelled for Lowelito to come and look. Clearly, we had again stumbled accidentally into a place of magic. We were surrounded by hills, up the sides of which were beautiful little houses of many colors winding along narrow cobblestone streets. And on top of each hill there was either a beautiful colonial church or chapel. At that moment, as Lowelito looked out onto this incredible sight, all the bells began to ring.

Going hurriedly out into the street, we were overwhelmed again by the beauty we were seeing and by the exciting, busy life of the people. We were not unaware of disagreeable odors, filth, and what appeared to be much human misery, since there were so many beggars about. Yet such bright and sparkling sunlight poured down over everything that even alleyways strewn with garbage were turned into visual magic. Since we were solely interested in the way things looked, we knew we were going to love this old city. So we found an apartment for rent and moved into it the same day.

*   *   *

The apartment we rented was on the top of a four-story building about a block from the cathedral. It was, in fact, a penthouse, although at that time we had never heard of a "penthouse." We soon learned that everybody in Guanajuato made much use of his rooftop. People would come out onto their roofs in the late afternoons to sit, just as the people of the Old South used to sit on their galleries. Even the prisoners in the large jail a few blocks from our apartment were permitted to come out onto the rooftop in the late afternoons. Often they would start singing to the whole city—to all their fellow citizens surrounding them on all the other rooftops.

In the street below our apartment, there was a dark hole in a wall, in which an old Indian lived. He sold charcoal and lived in that hole with his charcoal. Because of the blackness of the charcoal and the absence of light on the inside, it was not possible to see far back into the place, but at times this Indian would emerge from his dark cavern into the bright light at the entrance. He was not, however, black himself, except for his hair. His hands, face, and feet were an off-black. You could tell that his clothes had once been white. They were now the color white cloth becomes after long contact with charcoal. Odd as it may seem, that color is not black, the way we think of charcoal, but a very dull yellow ochre. The contrast between the brilliant sunlight outside and that dark hole with the Indian and charcoal inside fascinated me. I had once painted a picture of two charcoal burners coming down a steep mountainside behind the village of Ajijic, and I was interested in how different this man of charcoal in Guanajuato appeared.

A few blocks from our apartment, I had discovered a very steep, crooked, and narrow street that led up to a fabulously beautiful little blue chapel. From the miniature effect of the chapel, one might think it had been built by a race of fairy people. I carried my painting materials up to that little chapel and started a painting of it. Early each morning when I would go up the hill to paint it, I would meet Indians hurrying down toward the marketplace. The men wore the usual white *calzones*, and the women always had their heads and shoulders wrapped in gray *rebozos*. Those people would always give me a warm and friendly greeting when we met. One old woman, wrapped in a gray rebozo and carrying a basket of chickens on her head, would say as she made a sweeping, graceful, yet balanced, gesture, *"Beso la mano de usted, señor."* ("I kiss your hand, sir.")

Guanajuato, like most places in Mexico, had once been entirely a place of Indians, but after the Spaniards had conquered the Aztecs they had spread out in all directions. The Spaniards found gold and silver in Guanajuato, and after the colonial period the gold attracted a wide variety of non-Indian people—including Englishmen, Americans, Canadians, and even Irishmen. Most of the people who had been attracted by the gold, however, had long since departed when Lowelito and I arrived in Guanajuato and we certainly took no interest in the gold that might still be present in the mines. Lowelito commented that just as gold attracts some people, its absence repels them. We found that there were few foreigners in Guanajuato now that the gold and silver mines had become quite depleted. Lowelito and I were therefore somewhat unusual, in that the gold and silver in the mines had not attracted us, while their absence made the place more attractive to us.

One American still in Guanajuato lived in the hope that one rich vein of silver had been overlooked by all those earlier miners and that he would find it. His partner in this unpromising venture was a sixty-year-old Canadian gentleman named Mr. Newton, who at that time had been in Mexico for over thirty years. As I came to know Mr. Newton I grew to feel sympathetic toward him, for he struck me as being, in both manner and personality, a family man even though he had no family. He had a continual longing for one, and because of this he appeared to me a tragic figure.

"I was engaged to a beautiful schoolteacher in Toronto," he told me. "I had an opportunity to come to

Mexico, and it seemed to me then that in just one year I could make a fortune and return for my bride. We both agreed that I should do this, but I never went back. Oh, I did in time make a fortune, but I lost it. Then I made another and another, but in mining you also lose. I did not know this would happen to me. It is now too late. My life did not work out the way I wanted it to. Only recently have I realized that it is now too late."

It was clear to us that this Canadian gentleman felt he had been deeply tricked by life, and for this reason Lowelito and I were most sympathetic toward him. We both agreed that it must have been his inner longing for a family that caused him to dye his suit a bright red. It had become our custom to have lunch with him each noon in the main hotel in Guanajuato, and one day he showed up in this brilliant red suit, which he said he had dyed himself. He asked us what we thought of the color he had chosen. We did like the color and told him so. But the truth was that there was no other suit of clothes in all Guanajuato, or perhaps in all of Mexico, like his. But strange as it may seem, his new red suit made him harmonize with his surroundings. Although different from everyone else in his appearance, he no longer looked like a foreigner. He now might even have been taken for a Mexican. I think this was because his bright-red suit took him out of his former distinctly non-Mexican category.

Mr. Newton told us that he did not sleep well, but that it did not bother him at all since he would just turn on the light and read. He said that he had finished reading H. G. Wells's *Outline of History* and was now going through the Bible during his sleepless hours.

We were sure that all this was because of his unhappy bachelorhood.

In Guanajuato I became aware of one particular American attitude I regarded as deplorable and even embarrassing. Among the few Americans in Guanajuato at that time was one who seemed popular with the other Americans and at least comfortably secure with the Mexicans. In the hotel bar, he would say to his American acquaintances, as though the place were not filled with Mexicans, "This is a wonderful country. The only thing wrong with it is that Mexicans are so thick down here." He seemed to regard the Mexicans as unavoidable misfortunes he had to put up with, like bad weather. Whenever he sounded off in this way, Lowelito and I felt embarrassed, fearing the Mexicans would assume all Americans felt as this man did.

*　　*　　*

In 1925, the streetcars that ran from the Plaza de la Unión up to the *presa* (a dam built by the city) were pulled by a number of small mules. The little animals must have had a hard time of it pulling those streetcars up the hill, especially since the streets were paved with slick cobblestones. But on the way down, the mules' problem was to keep from getting run over by this object they had struggled so hard to pull up, and to which they were still attached. After the mules had pulled the vehicle with all their might up that steep, narrow, winding street, the streetcar then seemed to show its appreciation by chasing the little creatures clear down to the plaza. The noise created by these animals rushing madly to keep in advance of the streetcar that was rumbling behind them was most fortunate, for it served as a warning to anyone who might at that time be walking along a narrow segment of the street. Such pedestrians knew that they must get back to where the street was a little wider than the streetcar or else run the risk of being flattened into a form like the ancient pre-Spanish figurines found in the area.

In the mid-twenties, there were no American tourists in Guanajuato. The few Americans there were certainly not tourists. "Tourism" was not a part of the economy. Some of the American men in Guanajuato had become the husbands of Mexican women, whose beauty in that place seemed to me to be inevitable. It would have been odd not to find beautiful women in an enchanted city. Some of the Indian women were the essence of grace as they moved silently through those magic streets, and often we would see a lady of Spanish descent and culture whose appearance was breathtaking.

The dominating effect of beauty in Guanajuato, however, came from its streets, with their surprising spaces, and from the many colonial buildings that bordered them. To walk through those streets on a bright, sunny day was like hearing Chopin's music with your eyes. More than that, it was like being in among the musical notes of Chopin, stepping in and out between all the notes and musical patterns. I was thinking of this one morning when suddenly there appeared in front of me, framed in a half door, a man whose visual effect was as incongruous in that setting as the croaking of a bullfrog would be in the midst of a Chopin waltz.

This man's name was Luke Short, and if he had not

"gone native" it must have been for the same reason that an ostrich could never hope to go native in a community of canaries. His wife was Mexican, and she had children by a former marriage who were Mexican. His Mexican family had taken him to its heart. When they would all go in a group to the skating rink to sit and watch the young people skate on roller skates, it was evident that Luke Short was a bona fide member of the family, but he still looked like an ostrich sitting among a flock of canaries. It might have been this visual incongruity that caused him to have certain strange dreams, which he often described to me as we sat in the plaza. The one about the mummies impressed me most of all.

In a dimly lighted underground room at the Guanajuato Panteón (cemetery), a large group of frightening mummies was on view. I did not know why those mummies were there, but I had heard of them, and Lowelito and I went to see them. Luke Short had told us about them, because of the odd dreams he said he kept having. How many times Luke Short had seen the mummies he did not say, but to appreciate his dream one should have seen them at least once. They stood in long rows on low shelves in a narrow underground corridor, so that as you walked between them they appeared to be staring down at you. Some of them still had fragments of clothing hanging here and there about their dried bodies, and the general effect was so macabre that I could not understand why anyone would ever want to make a second trip to see them.

In Luke Short's dream, he had been given the assignment of feeding milk to those mummies from a baby's bottle with a rubber nipple on it. He said that in

his dream he had had to feed each and every one of
them by force. They would throw their heads back and
resist all the way down the line.

Perhaps it would become tiresome to tell about all
the people we met in Guanajuato, for their number
seems endless even though we made an effort not to
meet people at all. The Mexico we were interested in
was limited to that which was visible. It would have been
just as well for us had the inhabitants of Guanajuato
been deaf and dumb, as silent as the architecture, the
mountains, the sunlight, and the blue sky. It would have
suited us even more if, at the same time, we could have
been invisible.

The truth is that in Mexico one can learn all one is
capable of digesting merely through observation and
without the aid of verbal comment of any sort. But despite our lack of interest in personalities, there was no
escaping them. They revealed themselves to us in the
same irresistible way that dreams steal into the mind
during sleep. Unlike dreams, however, they have turned
out to be unforgettable. Two of the most unforgettable
of all happened to be two that we would gladly have
forgotten.

Our escape from the Philosopher in Chapala was a
complete success for a long, happy time, but we should
have known that this carefree existence could not last.
There was no philosopher in Guanajuato to interfere
with our work, which had nothing in common with philosophy, since philosophy can be done only with words.
For a while, therefore, Lowelito and I were free to pur-
sue our natural goals. But this fortunate situation was
not to last.

Early one bright, sunny morning, as we ascended

one of the hills along a pretty and winding narrow street in search of that perfect subject to draw and paint, there suddenly came alongside of us two young fellows who announced that they were students, that they wanted to learn English, and that they were coming along with us. We felt sunk, knowing that you can't draw or paint—or even see—while talking and socializing. These two boys really leeched onto us. They were as bad as two philosophers, and they brought our work to a sudden halt. Each day they would lie in wait for us. When finally we did not appear, thinking we might be able to do some work from memory indoors, they began coming to our apartment, just as the Chapala philosopher had done. These boys were Mexicans who knew only a little English, and they were determined to use us to master the English language.

One day they started in telling us about their English teacher, who had classes every Thursday night. "You must come and meet our teacher, Miss Hatch," they would say over and over. "When are you coming to meet Miss Hatch?" They kept this up for days, always asking us, "When are you coming to meet Miss Hatch?" It was bad enough to have met these boys, but the thought of being distracted from painting into teaching English was more than Lowelito could stand.

One morning, the boys arrived and the younger one got right onto the subject of Miss Hatch. "When are you coming to meet Miss Hatch?" he asked Lowelito. I think Lowelito must have been feeling worse than usual, for his answer not only surprised and shocked me but it was a great puzzle to the two Mexican boys. Lowelito said in a firm and determined voice, "Oh, fuck Miss Hatch!"

"Fuck Miss Hatch," the boy repeated excitedly. "*¿Qué quiere decir* 'fuck Miss Hatch'?" ("What does 'fuck Miss Hatch' mean?") The boys had never heard the word before and were now eager to know what it meant. They were now very excited to be about to learn some English that was entirely new to them.

I told Lowelito that it was up to him to explain the meaning since he was the one who said the word. So Lowelito began to explain, and his explanation shocked me again. He said that the word he used was a most friendly "salutation," and that it would make any woman, especially an English teacher, very pleased to hear it. He said if they would say at their next English class, "Fuck you, Miss Hatch," she would be inclined to give them an A in the course. I could hardly believe my ears. Lowelito was not like that. I told him he should not do such a thing.

The boys were apparently so eager to use their new English on their teacher that they left earlier than usual, in a very happy mood. I told Lowelito again that it was not at all like him to talk like that. But as it turned out, it was the best thing he could have done. We never knew what happened, but the boys never came back to study English with us after that. In fact, we never even saw them again.

*   *   *

The name Martínez is a common one among Mexicans. It is comparable to the name Smith in our country, so anyone who has spent some time in Mexico will surely have known many Martínezes. The first Martínez I ever knew was that one who peddled tamales up and down the streets of the East Texas town where I grew up. I knew him for many years, but I was never able to talk with him until after I was grown and had learned to speak Spanish. When that had happened, he and I became good friends, and he used to pose for me. I made many drawings and paintings of him. I think he was almost pure Aztec Indian. I have never found any tamales as good as the ones made by that Indian Martínez.

Of the other Martínezes I have known, two have been artists, both probably of pure Spanish descent. Ricardo Martínez is today one of the most imaginative and aesthetic painters in Mexico. The other was Alfredo Ramos Martínez, whose name will always be known and respected in the history of Mexican art. Alfredo Ramos, like Fra Angelico, did not know how to see anything as ugly. Assuming that something he looked at was actually ugly, he would unconsciously discover or imagine relationships of space and color within it which would make it beautiful. He was a close friend of mine.

But the Martínez I knew in Guanajuato was not outstanding as the others I mention were. He was no artist and he could not make tamales. But he certainly could speak the English language as well as I could, although he was definitely a Mexican, of the mestizo type. You had only to look at him to know that his ancestors were both Indian and Spanish. One of the interesting things about him, however, was that he owned a flock of bilingual parrots. Lowelito said that they were actually trilingual, since in addition to speaking English and Spanish they would at times lapse into a language of their own, which had nothing to do with either English or Spanish. When we sat in Señor Martínez's patio, the noise of those birds was on all sides, and such words as "good morning," "adiós," "Polly wants a cracker," "¡*válgame Dios*!"—and others too bad to mention—were mingled with words of their own native tongue.

Those parrots of Señor Martínez, insofar as what they talked about, must surely have been a revelation of his own personality. Whatever they knew how to say, they had picked up from him. Lowelito said they were like Señor Martínez's own children, and that parents have a great influence on their children and that what we were hearing was as though Señor Martínez himself were saying it. I did not agree with that. I reminded Lowelito that, regardless of parental influence, every child eventually turns out to be unique and never says exactly the sentences his parents say. But Lowelito said that that was not true of parrots. "Señor Martínez's parrots," Lowelito insisted, "only say exactly what Señor Martínez says." Lowelito added that Señor Martínez ought to blush every time his parrots opened their beaks. I told him that it was a good thing we didn't have a parrot in the room when he told those boys what to say to Miss Hatch. But in any case it was clear that Señor Martínez believed that his parrots were themselves responsible for what they said, so instead of blushing, he was amused. But he certainly never scolded them. In the end, however, his educated parrots got him into trouble.

There was a widow in Guanajuato at that time for whom Señor Martínez had tender feelings. She also owned parrots, which may have been the reason that Señor Martínez came to meet her. This lady suddenly learned that she had to go to Mexico City for a prolonged period of time, and Señor Martínez graciously offered to take care of her parrots while she was away.

"They will be no trouble at all," he assured her. "They can just move right in with my birds."

After this widow's parrots arrived, the parrot talk was for a while much more varied, and perhaps even more polite. But, as it turned out, we all learned that one should be careful with whom he lets his parrots associate. Señor Martínez certainly did not have a bad influence on the widow's parrots, but his own parrots seemed to go in for teaching their guests all they knew, which of course was what they had learned from Señor Martínez. According to him, his parrots taught the widow's parrots so thoroughly that the visitors adopted their new knowledge and discarded or forgot everything they had learned from living with the widow.

With some uneasiness Lowelito and I helped Señor Martínez deliver the widow's parrots to her when she returned from Mexico City a couple of months later. We had never quite believed what he had told us about the widow's parrots learning bad words from his parrots, so when we helped release her birds into their old home cage we were pleased to note that they were chattering in their native tongue. But just as we were closing the cage door, to our amazement one of the widow's biggest parrots, a yellow-headed one named Panchita, let out a terrible screech, flew up on a perch, and, turning her head so that she could look at the widow, screamed in a loud and clear voice: "'Son of a bitch!' cried Daniel." We did not know whether the widow spoke English or not, but Lowelito and I thought that we had better leave, which we did without being introduced to the widow.

We often wondered after that what the widow did with her corrupted parrots, assuming that they really were corrupted, as Señor Martínez and the evidence we

had heard suggested they were. We had been told by
Señor Martínez that the widow was a deeply religious
woman, and Lowelito said that she probably would take
the birds with her to confession. We never discussed
those parrots with Señor Martínez again, and he never
mentioned the widow to us again.

During those months in Guanajuato, we learned
that a matchmaker who speaks Spanish is about the same
as one whose language is English, and that her tech-
nique with Cupid's bow and arrow is also about the same.

That we understood Spanish so poorly then was not
the slightest hindrance to our landlady Cata, who would
talk to us as though we were only joking about not understanding all she was saying. She would say that she
was just dying for us to meet not only her daughter but
also "the dear little friend of her dear little daughter."
However, this landlady of ours was, unlike Luke Short, a
person of restraint, manners, and respect for conven-
tion. Luke Short had said bluntly the day we encoun-
tered him there in the midst of Chopin's music, "Now, if
you want to learn Spanish, the only way to do it is to get
yourselves a couple of sleeping dictionaries." We soon
noticed, however, that the dictionary he was sleeping
with was also his wife, and according to him, she dis-
turbed his beauty sleep each morning before daybreak
when she left his warm bed to go to Mass.

Cata in those days would put fruit on our apartment table, and whenever we surprised her in the act
she would say that she especially wanted Lowelito to
meet "*la amiguita de mi hijita*" because they were just the
right size for each other. From that I surmised that her
own daughter must be quite tall, like me. Then one day
we received from Cata a formal invitation to come to
her *salón*.

Her *salón* was on the floor below our penthouse, somewhere deep back in the interior of the building. The building itself, with its many balconies and inner patios, was a mystery to us.

On the day appointed for our presence in the *salón* of Cata, our chief concern was to look our best, so I wore a coat. Lowelito at that time did not own a coat, but he did have a button-up sweater and he wore that. We were now going to a party of a kind we had not known before. We had been to parties in Chapala, but they had been spontaneous gatherings where liquor took the place of women and all was extremely informal. As we descended from our penthouse to Cata's apartment, we did not know whether or not there would be liquor, but we were prepared to expect women.

We proceeded through several corridors untl we arrived at the *salón*. It was a long room and we entered through a door near the end of one of the long walls. Cata seemed to be on roller skates as she approached us and led us toward the other end of the room. There in front of us were two rows of straight chairs facing each other about four feet apart. In the chairs on one side were already seated three beautiful Mexican girls. Cata took her place on the feminine side, while Lowelito and I sat in the chairs opposite.

It was an excellent arrangement for carrying on a conversation. The absence of a table between us seemed to lay us wide open. I have since thought that if conference tables were eliminated it might make a great difference in the way people acted and thought, even among diplomats.

Looking right across in front of us at those beautiful señoritas with flashing black eyes seemed to cause me to forget what little Spanish I knew, and of course

Lowelito knew almost none to begin with. The girls did not know any English at all. Before long, however, we had discovered some common ground, which made us speak to each other in our two languages without being at all concerned with the mere problem of communication. The whole room was abuzz, and I was contributing my full share to the sound when suddenly something happened that had the effect of lifting me completely out of the stream of talk, for now I could say no more, or, at best, talk only in a mechanical way.

There at the far end of the room, a door began to open ever so slowly, until it reached a certain point. Then it slowly closed. This happened several times. I became aware that something or somebody was watching us. Then I caught a glimpse of what it was—or rather, how it looked. At this point, I recalled how the ancient Indians, as well as the Spaniards, used to keep monstrosities in their households as a kind of entertainment. As I got other glimpses of this creature back in the semidarkness behind the door—and apparently I was the only one of our group who had seen it—I began to hope that it was chained, for quite obviously it could open and close the door. Moreover, it soon became clear to me that it was taking great delight in having diverted my attention from the others. With its grimacings and what seemed to me to be some sort of strange insults, it was trying to hold my attention. In this it was succeeding extremely well, for I had now become a participant in an entirely different party in Cata's *salón*.

*   *   *

All the time Lowelito and I were in Guanajuato, we did not take much interest in facts about that old city.

We could not get our minds off the way everything
looked. What meets the eye and ear on all sides in that
city is so rich and absorbing that even a statistician would
probably forget his profession and be content to contemplate the immediate scene. That there lies below
that scene endless material for interpretation, there can
be no doubt. But the viewpoint of the artist, which causes
him to regard all things as sufficient in themselves, is
certain to prevail in Guanajuato.

There was one fact, however, that Lowelito and I
could not ignore. It was the precise location of our penthouse, in all six directions: east and west, north and
south, and up and down. Our penthouse was situated at
the base of a high and steep cliff. On special religious
and patriotic occasions those Mexicans who considered
holidays a time to celebrate in a truly effective manner
would assemble on top of that cliff.

Among those celebrators were some who had access
to an endless supply of dynamite. An American miner
told me this dynamite was stolen from the mines, but
knowing the attitude of Mexicans toward holidays I am
convinced that "stolen" is the wrong word to apply to
their possession of that explosive material. The sticks
of dynamite may have been removed from the mines
quietly, but it would seem incorrect to say that what is
done for the honor of mankind, or the love of Mexico,
or for the glory of God, could possibly involve theft.

But stolen or not, those sticks of dynamite could not
be ignored, especially by those down below them when
they began flying through the air and exploding with
deafening noise. Our penthouse was so situated that if
the dynamite did not explode high up, it would then
explode near, and possibly within, the penthouse. Sometimes it appeared that the Mexicans up above were try-

ing to interest us in a sort of relay game, in which our part was to give those sticks that reached us still fizzing a new start on down the hill.

In contrast to the noise of the dynamite was the sound of the church bells, which had a soothing effect so different from the jarring one of explosions. Fortunately the explosions came only on holidays, while the bells rang out—all over the city—every hour. In between the ringing of the bells, one might become vividly aware of silence, especially if he was upon some hillside overlooking the city. The silence he would then notice would seem to be a part of the brilliant white sunlight, and even a part of the view of the city below. On those hillsides around Guanajuato grew many big tree-cactus plants, which produced a little dark red berry called *garambulla*. When ripe, this berry had an unforgettably delicious flavor. Lowelito said that it was not only the sunlight but also the view of the city that went into the making of that unique flavor. He said that the berries on those cactus trees over the hill, where there was no view, did not have as good a taste as the ones that could see the city down below them.

This blending of things may be a part of the secret of the strange spell of Guanajuato. For there sounds have a way of seeming integrated with colors, while colors seem not to exist apart from textures and solidarities. Just as the old city allows the hills and the sky a full share in its total effect, so the people of Guanajuato refuse to make separate compartments out of time. Were it not for this, those little processions led to the Panteón by a barefoot father carrying on his head a little blue coffin would be altogether too tragic to be seen as having beauty of any sort.

*　　*　　*

All the time I was in Guanajuato, I was receiving letters from that black-haired girl up in California. It seemed to me, and I thought maybe to her also, that we were getting to like each other very much. But since all this had come about through the written word and without the use of our eyes, I felt I should go back to the States and look into her eyes and let her look into mine. So I told Lowelito that I was going to be leaving for a short time. He thought I should do that, but seemed to be worried how he would be able to buy cigarettes without my help. His Spanish, if anything, had stagnated in Guanajuato.

Lowelito decided that since he would be without an interpreter for a while he had better go back to Chapala and find Isidoro. He did not know how he was going to handle the philosopher, but he thought he would feel more secure in Chapala, anyway. We packed up our things, putting mine in my steamer trunk, and Lowelito's in his two suitcases. I then went with Lowelito to the railroad station and saw him leave for Chapala. I was to leave the next morning at daybreak and catch a train north at the town of Silao, some thirty miles away.

When I returned to the penthouse apartment after seeing Lowelito off that afternoon, I came up my stairway very suddenly. I had left my trunk completely packed and securely tied up with ropes. As I came into the room, there in the middle of the floor was my trunk upside down, and squatting upon it like a monkey was an Indian with his back to me. He was cutting the bottom out of the trunk with a large machete. The blows he was wielding so furiously were making so much noise that he had not heard my approach, and the splinters were flying about as though he were felling a tree. In my astonishment at his industry, I was slow in announcing my presence. When I did, the Indian dashed out onto the flat roof and I after him. He circled around and made the stairway ahead of me. I lost sight of him before we reached the street below, but the color of his feet and hands—and those dull yellow ochre clothes he wore—were enough for me to know that this was the man of the charcoal, the one who lived in that dark hole in the wall. Later that same afternoon, to my surprise, this Indian came to my apartment. He told me that he had heard I was leaving on the train the next morning and that he would like to have the job of carrying my trunk to the railroad station. It was with mingled emotions that I agreed and that I watched him repair the hole he had cut into it. At daybreak next morning, I tried to keep up with him as he trotted through the streets with my trunk on his back, for I could not help fearing that the trunk might find its way into some other dark hole in a wall. But he discharged his contract with honesty, and I felt that he really meant it when he wished that God would go with me on my journey.

3
Ajijic

In the year 1925, the general public was not traveling about in airplanes. Lindbergh had not yet flown across the Atlantic Ocean. If one needed to travel a long distance by land, the best way to go was by railroad train. There were automobiles, but the roads to travel were mostly unpaved and rough, especially in Mexico. In addition, automobile tires were so poorly made that even on short trips by car one could expect any number of blowouts. So my trip back to visit that black-haired girl was to be a long one by train: first in a Mexican train to the Texas border, and then in an American train on west. In order to break the long journey, I decided to go by my old hometown in Texas. From there I would continue on to Tucson, Arizona, for that was where I would find the object of my visit. She had recently left her newspaper job in California, and had gone to study at the University of Arizona.

When I arrived in my Texas hometown, I was told by a boyhood friend that if I would come back through on my return trip to Mexico, he thought he might be able to go down there with me. I did not like traveling alone, and I was not then at all sure when my black-haired girl friend would accompany me, if ever.

Since this is a story about what I saw and did in Mexico over several years, I shall not dwell long on what happened to me in Tucson, Arizona. Reaching that little city very early in the morning, I telephoned that girl, and was told to wait in the station, that she would be there in time to have breakfast with me.

"I shall be wearing a light blue dress," she said.

That information was not necessary, I felt, although it had been a long time since I had seen her.

The dress she was wearing when she arrived was a light gray-blue, and her hair was truly as black as a raven's wing. I will add that before I left Tucson in a few days my feet were just barely touching the ground. They were carrying me places, but they no longer made good contact with the earth. It was quite obvious to me that what had begun to happen to me by mail was real.

I do not know why I did it, but I asked her if she would like to go out in the desert with me to make a painting. It was not to impress upon her that I was an artist. Perhaps it was because I had become so accustomed to painting every day that I could not stop.

She went with me, and as I painted, or tried to paint, she talked a blue streak. Finally, I said to her, "Look, I simply can't paint while you are talking. If you want me to make this painting, you will have to keep quiet for a while." That could have put an end to our developing relationship, but fortunately, she told me later, she was impressed and pleased by my outspokenness.

The reason I could not paint while she talked was not that what she said distracted me. It was the sound of her voice. To this day, I find it difficult to notice what she is saying because of giving my attention solely to the beauty of her voice. Sometimes she accuses me of not listening. The fact is that I do listen, but not to her words. I listen to the musical sounds of her voice. I cannot help that.

*   *   *

When I arrived back in my Texas hometown, I went out to see my boyhood friend. His name was Traynham Pitts, and he was then working on an oil-drilling rig. I went out to see him where the oil well was being drilled. The high derrick stood alone in a field of cotton that had been picked over. There were no other oil derricks in sight, for this was a wildcat well. He told me they were about to bring in a gusher, but that did not affect his plans at all. The way he walked off from his job at that drilling operation convinced me that he would like Mexico. He did not speak to anyone on the rig. He just took off his gloves, shut off the fire under the boiler he was tending, and got into my car. He said he had saved up enough money. The name Traynham Pitts had always seemed unusual to me, and for that reason it was just right for him, since he was an unusual person. After leaving high school, he had joined the merchant marine. His experiences had been varied, and perhaps unusual also.

We left immediately by train, crossing the Mexican border at Laredo, Texas. We missed our connections at Querétaro and had to spend the night in a hotel in that old city of colonial churches. The little plaza in front of the hotel was colorful, with great bougainvillaea vines in brilliant purple bloom. Flitting about the vines were large black jackdaws that filled the air with their jarring squawks. The next day we arrived in Guadalajara and went immediately to Chapala by the little train.

When we arrived in Chapala, Lowelito gave me the good news that the Philosopher had gone away. Lowelito had rented a small house for us in the village of Ajijic, down the dirt road from Chapala.

Lowelito and I were the first art students ever to live in Ajijic. Years later this beautiful little native village on the lake would become a gathering spot of American artists, writers, marijuana smokers, and American lady schoolteachers on vacation. Eventually, real-estate promoters would move in, and hordes of American tourists would arrive. But all of this development was still years away when we lived there.

The first thing I did upon my arrival in Chapala was to go to the general-delivery window at the post office, for I was eager to hear from that black-haired girl. She had told me she would soon give me a date—or not give me a date—for joining me in Mexico. After I had read the letter that was handed me, my feet again left the earth. I walked on Mexican air from the post office back to the plaza, where Lowelito and Traynham Pitts were seated on a bench.

"I have a letter from Eileen," I said. "She says she can marry me on July 21st, and will meet me for that purpose in El Paso. That means I will have about six months with you guys in Ajijic. But of course I will bring her back here with me."

Perhaps if I had been intelligent, I would never have considered getting married, for I had no way of supporting a wife. I thought my income at that time would be adequate for Mexico; however, it would run out, in about a year. Then it would be up to God to take care of us. I mentioned this to Lowelito, and he assured me that everything would work out all right. He also said it was not up to me to think of things like that, anyway—that what we do in this world is never our own fault. "We are all at the mercy of evolution," he said.

* * *

The house Lowelito had rented in Ajijic was on the narrow street that ran through the village and on to Jocotepec, at the end of the lake. As in Chapala, all the houses in Ajijic were joined together, forming a solid continuous wall that staggered down the street, with a narrow sidewalk between the wall and street. Our house had several rooms, including one large one on the street side. In the thick adobe walls of this big room, there were two large windows opening onto the street, and beyond the windows a wide door that opened into an entrance hallway. The hallway led back to our patio, which was behind the big room. This house was adequate as living quarters for the three of us, but as a place to paint and draw it was not so good. I began immediately to search for a second house, which would serve as a studio, and I found such a place only a block away.

The house I found and rented seemed about perfect. It consisted of just one large room with an entrance hallway next to it. The hallway led into a back yard, or patio, behind the room. A wide double door opened from the room onto that patio, and when the doors were open they let lots of light into the room. The floor of the room was paved with rough, worn ten-inch-square red tiles. The patio was enclosed by a high stone wall, and at the back of the patio, near the wall, there were two trees. One was an orange tree laden with small sour oranges. The other was a pomegranate tree filled with beautiful deep red pomegranates.

Lowelito had already hired a woman to cook for us twice a day and to do our laundry. Her name was Angela. She had two pretty daughters. The older one, about fifteen, was named Paz, and the younger one, about ten, had the name María de la Luz Blanca. Paz was such a beautiful Indian type, with her black hair braided with blue ribbons, that I had her sit for me. I made several small paintings of her graceful head.

One bright morning at our studio, Traynham Pitts was reading in the sunny patio just outside the open doorway, while I was busy inside painting Paz. I would have her hold very still about fifteen minutes at a time, and then I would tell her to rest for a few minutes. Paz seemed to be amused each time I told her to rest, for she considered that she had been resting all the time she was holding still posing. So I decided to let her continue posing for about a half hour before telling her to rest. Suddenly, to my amazement, she said very clearly, and so loudly that Traynham heard her, "Oh, shit!" Traynham came running in. He asked excitedly and hopefully if Paz spoke English. I assured him that she didn't, that that was the only English word she knew. Little Paz could not speak English at all, so I asked her who had taught her that word, and if she knew what it meant. She answered that a boy who had worked on the railroad tracks in the United States had taught her that word, and that it meant, "I am tired." I told her that it did not mean, "I am tired," and that it was a bad word which she should never say again.

In some ways Ajijic in 1926 was very different from Chapala. At that time, neither village was well known to Americans. We were the only Americans living in Ajijic, just as we had been in Chapala. However, Chapala was a place that attracted Mexican vacationers, while Ajijic was in no way a resort. People did not come there from Guadalajara over weekends, as they did to Chapala. Also, there seemed to be more native "characters" in

Ajijic. One young woman, who was always around, was a deaf-mute. We had not been there long when we learned that she had put out the story that she was sleeping often not only with the *presidente municipal* and the local priest, but also with Traynham Pitts. This girl was always dirty-looking, in her black dress and old, worn gray rebozo. When Traynham learned of the story she had spread about him, he was very upset. He said the thought that he would even get near that creature made him sick. I assured him that it was only the poor girl's way of attracting attention to herself. With such stories going around nobody could ignore her.

One morning, a young Indian boy walked into our studio singing a religious song. He was an odd-looking boy, with big round eyes that appeared to be about to pop out, and he was wearing a bright-pink shirt. Lowelito thought that he might be a good subject to draw, so he had him pose. But the boy wouldn't stop singing, and when a person is singing at the top of his voice, it is difficult to make a drawing or painting of him. This boy said he worked for the priest in Jocotepec. He was very religious. We found it hard to get him to stop singing long enough to talk, but he did eventually tell us that there was a crucifix statue in a church in Jocotepec carved from the root of a tree. He added that it was black and extremely sacred.

We had not yet been as far down the road as Jocotepec. It was at least twelve miles from Ajijic—too far to walk and get back in one day. But Lowelito insisted that we should go to Jocotepec and see that black statue.

I went to see the *presidente municipal*, for I knew he owned some burros. He lived so near us that the braying of his donkeys was a daily serenade. It turned out that

this man also owned a couple of little black mules, the kind whose father was a male burro, or jack, and whose mother was a female horse, or mare. I arranged to rent two of the burros and one little mule for the daylong trip to Jocotepec.

When we went after those animals, I noticed that the little black mule was livelier than the two donkeys. I also noticed that the mayor of Ajijic gave us two long needles for the burros, but no needle at all for the mule. The purpose of the long needles was to prod the donkeys on their rear ends to make them speed up. Traynham obviously wanted to ride the mule, so Lowelito and I gladly chose the burros. They were different from the black mule, but there was no difference between them. As far as I could see, they might have been twins.

We started out early in the morning, going slowly through the village cobblestone street and continuing onto the dirt road that led to Jocotepec. I had always thought that nothing was more beautiful than a dirt road, and this one leading along the lake to Jocotepec was especially beautiful. It was actually a lane, for it was enclosed on both sides by continuous rock fences. All

the rocks that must once have littered the fields on both
sides of the road had been gathered up and made into
these fences. Here and there along the fences were
great clumps of prickly-pear cactus. Now and then we
would come to fairly large trees growing along the
fences. In the fields on the lake side of the road, we
could see row after row of tree-melon (papaya) trees extending down to the lake, and beyond these strange
trees, with their melons attached at the tops of the
trunks, were fields of *chayotes*, a most amazing vegetable,
whose plant grows so fast you can almost see it move
along.

The morning was bright and beautiful, with a few
white clouds scattered above us in the blue sky. As we
went slowly down this lane, I noticed that the silent
shadows from the clouds above seemed to be going along
to Jocotepec with us. Because of the varying intensity of
the sunlight, the shadows seemed to be breathing as
they moved along. On our left, beyond the fields, we
could see the great gray expanse of the lake, and on our
right, mountains rose up sharply. Those were the mountains Lowelito, Isidoro, and I were climbing when we
saw the charcoal burners coming down loaded with
wood with which to make charcoal—a subject I painted
before going to Guanajuato.

Twelve miles on the back of a slow-moving burro, if
you are not accustomed to it, can grow tiresome to the
muscles. When we rode into the village of Jocotepec and
dismounted, I noticed that my entire body felt stiff.
Tying the burros to a post in the plaza, we decided to
find the church by walking. We still had twelve more
miles to cover in the afternoon.

Traynham Pitts had practically fallen in love with

his mule. He had arrived in Jocotepec ahead of Lowelito and me, and now was prancing around the plaza on his mule as though he were taking part in a horse show.

We found the crucifix statue in the church to be an interesting piece of primitive sculpture. Obviously some Indian had noticed that the form of a tree root with two branches above and one below had something in common with the form of a man's body. He had imagined just how to carve it here and there to bring about a closer resemblance, and then he had painted it black and attached it to a crude cross. I understood that Indian's way of thinking, for I had discovered that in painting it is much easier to imagine a form after some lines and shapes have been put on the canvas. The imagination, or the ability to visualize, needs some extra, outside help, at least in my case.

After having lunch in a little restaurant on the plaza we mounted our noble steeds and started back up the road to Ajijic. Traynham, always in the lead on his little black mule, was exploring both sides of the lane, back and forth, like a working bird dog. On this trip, the two donkeys Lowelito and I were riding seemed to require less prodding with the needles. Lowelito explained that it was because they realized we were now returning home. As we continued up the lane between the rock fences, now and then we would meet a giant longhorn steer moving so aimlessly and stopping so often that he seemed to be lost. We would also meet barefoot native women coming down the lane toward Jocotepec. Wrapped in their dark gray-blue rebozos, these women stepped gracefully and silently among the cloud shadows on the lane. Everyone who passed saluted us with "adiós," which not only meant "good-bye," but also "may you go with God." Everything visible along this lane belonged to, or contributed to, an overall harmony. I had the feeling that I was a part of that harmony, and that so was the burro carrying me.

By the time we had traveled six or seven miles up the narrow lane, the sun was getting down near the edge line of the high mountains to our left. Looking far ahead, I saw a cloud of dust that filled the lane from fence to fence. It was moving slowly toward us. Traynham Pitts, who was by now far ahead of us, rode his mule right into the dust cloud and disappeared. A moment after he disappeared in the cloud of dust, I could see that the dust was being churned up by a huge herd of burros, which completely filled the narrow lane. The burros were being herded by several Indians wearing their dusty white *calzones* and red sashes.

Since Traynham had apparently passed successfully through the wave of donkeys on his mule, I assumed I would have no difficulty getting through on my burro, and, to my relief, my little animal did weave its way in and out among all those burros, as though they were only so many bushes. But that was not the way it turned out for Lowelito. Seeing me enter the herd, he must have decided to wait and see how I came out, for when I had cleared the entire herd I looked back and saw that Lowelito was just beginning to enter it. He had not gone far into the midst of the burros, however, when a great disturbance broke out. So much dust was being kicked up that I could not see exactly what was happening. The burros now seemed to be going in circles, making lots of noise with their hooves, and some were even braying. Lowelito began to yell for me to come back and get him out. But I did not see how I could possibly do that. For a while, the disturbance was a puzzle to me, but soon I understood. Through the cloud of dust, Lowelito could be glimpsed clinging desperately to the back and neck of his burro as that beast lunged with front feet high in the air onto the back of first one female donkey and then another. Lowelito said later that he was afraid to dismount for fear of being trampled by all those donkey hooves, which he said he remembered were four times as many as all the donkeys around him.

Lowelito's burro had turned out to be a very virile male, or jack, and he was attempting to make love to all those jennies surrounding him. My own donkey apparently was a well-behaved female. So there was a much greater difference between our two donkeys than we had thought, and I knew that on any future trips we might have to flip a coin to see who would ride the jenny, and who the jack.

* * *

All the paintings I had finished were now in Ajijic, including the early ones of the Guadalajara cemetery, the Chapala ones, and those I had made in Guanajuato. Since they were all on canvas, it would be easy to roll them into a small package. I was going to start a new life soon with my black-haired bride, and it seemed to me that I should ship the premarital paintings back to the States. The ones I would do in the future would surely be a lot better, and the old ones should not be around to remind me of my past struggles.

I rolled the paintings and wrapped and tied them thoroughly. I then took them to Chapala, since the mail arrived there before going on down the dirt road to Ajijic. At the Chapala post office, I handed the package through the window and asked how many stamps it needed.

When the mailman, who turned out to be the postmaster, took the package, he looked it over, turned it around, and then asked, "What is in this package?"

"Art," I answered. "Pictures, paintings."

"We shall have to look at them," he said. And he began to cut my strings and unwrap the package.

At first he only scattered the paintings around on a table, at different angles, with some partly overlapping others. But soon it became evident that he was an art critic, for he began to tack the paintings up on the walls all around the post office, and to contemplate each one separately.

Of the eighteen or twenty pictures that were in the package, the postmaster said that only three could be mailed through his post office. So I took them all back with me to Ajijic. I might have been very discouraged by this post-office critic had it not been clear to me that his judgment had been based altogether upon subject matter. In fact, he had given me a lecture on what I should paint. He said that those straw shacks of the Indians I had painted would give the wrong impression about Mexico, and that I should paint Spanish señoritas, especially if I wanted to mail my paintings back to the United States. That incident had been my first confrontation with an art jury, and I had come off very poorly: my work had been turned down.

*   *   *

When I got back to Ajijic with my package of rejected paintings, I went straight to our studio, unlocked

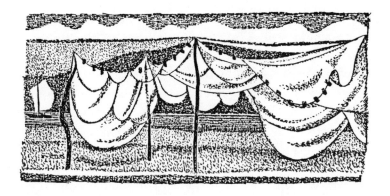

the entrance door, and put the paintings on a table in-side. I was surprised not to find Traynham or Lowelito there, for it was still only midafternoon. Going out into the patio, I noticed that the orange tree, which had been loaded with fruit, was completely stripped. Not a single orange was left on the tree. I could not imagine how all those oranges had disappeared so quickly. But when I arrived at our house on the main street of Ajijic, I soon found the answer to that puzzle. Both windows opening onto the street were wide open and the street was lit-tered with orange peels. A mariachi band was playing inside our big room, and people were coming down the street and going into our patio. They were nearly all In-dians. I was still puzzled as I followed them in. But what I saw there was beginning to make some sense. Trayn-ham was standing on the far side of a table, and in front of him was a very large pot, or *olla*. On both sides of the *olla* were many bottles of tequila.

When Traynham saw me, he waved a bottle in the air and said, "We are giving a party! We have invited everybody in Ajijic to come."

He was working so hard, mixing orange juice and tequila in the big *olla* and passing out drinks to all com-

ers, that soon he took off his shirt and tossed it high
onto a side wall. The Indians seemed to love that gesture, which they must have taken as a sign of welcome,
for they kept coming with their glasses.

Traynham then sent Lowelito to get more tequila.
Mariachi music was filling the air, helping to attract
more guests. Lowelito returned with about six bottles of
tequila and then went out again immediately, before I
could talk to him. When he returned the second time,
he was carrying a large basket full of pomegranates. Apparently he had gone and stripped our pomegranate
tree at the other house. He gave the pomegranates to
Traynham, who began to crush them and let the juice
fall into the *olla* with the orange juice and tequila.

By nightfall, the party had warmed up. All parts of
the house and the patio were filled with Indians drinking Traynham's punch and singing to the music of the
mariachi.

Traynham must have mixed a stiff drink, for I do
not remember when the party came to an end.

The next morning, I was awakened by a loud knocking on our entrance door. When I opened it, I saw the
chief of police, the village *comandante*, standing there
with a wide straw sombrero on his head and framed by a
street full of yellow orange peels.

"Señor," he said, "I have come to collect the money
for the permit."

"What permit?" I asked him.

"Señor," he said, "you are required to obtain a permit to give a *gallo*, but since you did not know that, it is
all right for you to buy the permit after the *gallo*, in this
case."

We certainly had not known of that custom of buy-

Fishermen's Shacks, Chapala

The Charcoal Burners

ing a permit before giving a stag party, and we felt lucky that we could buy it after the fact. I did know that the party Traynham and Lowelito had cooked up had been a spontaneous one.

*   *   *

All the guests at the *gallo* had been the "Indians" of Ajijic. Although they all must have had some Spanish genes, they continued to look like their pure Indian ancestors. We were sure of this, because they looked so much like the pre-Spanish figurines found in that area. They were not at all like the people of Mescala, who disliked strangers. The Indians of Ajijic were friendly. In 1926, we were the only foreigners living in the village, and we felt very much at home. If any progress had ever come to Ajijic, it certainly didn't show at that time. Everything about the place, including the way the people lived, was beautiful. It seemed incredible to us that it would ever change.

After I had paid the village *comandante* for the permit to have a *gallo*, which we had already had, I closed the big entrance door and went back to tell Lowelito and Traynham what had happened. But before I could finish my story about the permit, someone began knocking on our door again. When I opened it, there stood before me this time a man I would never have expected. He was a young American.

"I am Henry Whitaker," he said. "I have just driven my car down all the way from Los Angeles." He was smiling like a cat that had just caught a mouse. He went on to say that he had to have his car ferried over several rivers. "But I made it," he continued. "I have proved that it can be done, and you fellows won't be so isolated after this."

Traynham and Lowelito had heard us talking, and they came to the door. Lowelito was friendly to this young American, but Traynham never said a word, and I saw him looking with squinted eyes at the young man all the time he was talking and bragging about his great feat.

When this adventurer had left, Traynham shook his head from side to side and said, "If we let this guy go, if we let him go back to Los Angeles, that will be the end of what we like about Mexico. In no time at all, they'll be coming down here by the thousands. We must knock him out and throw him in the lake. Isidoro will help us do it." Traynham also said that sooner or later the road would be paved clear down to Ajijic from Los Angeles, and real-estate developers would move in.

We certainly did not do what Traynham recommended, but I was not at all sure he was joking.

A couple of days later, Isidoro showed up with a friend Lowelito had met in Chapala when he returned from Guanajuato. This man's name was Alfredo Padilla. I liked him at once. He was in his late twenties, and he owned a little drugstore in Chapala.

Alfredo said there was going to be an interesting fiesta in the village of San Antonio that same day. He said we should go and see it because there would be some native dances in front of the church there. Since it was now nearly noon, I got Angela, our cook, to make us a quick, light lunch, and then Lowelito, Traynham, Isidoro, Alfredo, and I started up the dirt road to San Antonio, which was between Ajijic and Chapala.

On arriving in that village, we found the dances

going on in the churchyard, as Alfredo had told us they would be. Some of the Indians were dressed as Spanish conquistadores and others as Aztec Indians. There was a great crowd of people all around, and it seemed to me they were all drunk. Suddenly, about twenty feet from me, I saw two drunken Indians engaged in a friendly struggle for possession of a large pistol. They were obviously not angry with each other, for they were laughing uproariously as they struggled for the gun. But, even so, as the big pistol would sweep down in the grasp of one Indian while the other tried to get his own hands on it, it would go off, and its bullets would churn up the dust among the spectators. The crowd, seeing the danger, began to disperse. People were trying to get away from the drunken and playful Indians as fast as they could run. The bullets continued to stir up the dust all around. The five of us felt fortunate that we had not been hit by one of the stray bullets. We had already put a good distance between ourselves and those Indians with the gun, and we decided it would be wise to keep going on back to Ajijic.

* * *

All this social life had been interfering with my painting, and I was beginning to feel guilty. So I set up my easel about two blocks from the village church and started painting a street scene. I had been looking at that subject for several days, and I now felt that I knew just how it should be painted. A long wall went diagonally up the street from where my easel was located. It ended in an adobe house with a red-tile roof, and across the next street was a row of similar houses with red-tile roofs. Rising from behind the wall was a row of tremendous trees, but unlike the trees that I was trying to paint when the Russian woman nearly ran over me, the trunks of these trees were completely bare until they reached a great height. Behind all this, the blue-violet mountains back of Ajijic rose up. The way I saw that subject had little to do with the way a camera or an Impressionist would have shown it, but nevertheless, I was definitely seeing it in a true way. What I was seeing was certainly there, and when I had finished that painting I knew that I had made it the way I had seen it. And I also discovered that I was no longer the same kind of Impressionist I had been before.

*   *   *

Nearly six months had passed since I came back to Chapala after my visit with the black-haired girl. And more than three years had gone by since Lowelito and I arrived for the first time in Guadalajara. My trip up to El Paso to meet Eileen was very much on my mind. I began to realize that a house would have to be found for our new life together. The one Lowelito had rented in Ajijic was much too small for all of us.

Since all the houses in Ajijic seemed to be about the same size, I decided that I had better look in Chapala. Lowelito and Traynham said they would go with me to look. I then went over to see the *presidente municipal,* and I again rented those two donkeys and the little black mule. But this time I decided to let Traynham Pitts ride on the of the burros. I would ride the mule. Traynham knew at once which burro was the jack, and he chose that one, to Lowelito's delight.

In Chapala, I had very good luck. For thirty-five dollars a month, I managed to rent an impressive ruin on the lakeshore. It was El Manglar, the house President Porfirio Díaz used to visit before he was forced into exile. This house, although run-down, was pretty—and it was large. It had a bathroom, and a kitchen with a giant old wood-burning cookstove. I also engaged a cook on that day. Her name was Margarita. She had a big family, a husband who was a drunkard, and three goats.

Being perfectly ready now for Eileen, we started back to Ajijic on our mule and donkeys. While I was renting the house, Lowelito and Traynham had acquired a bottle of alcohol mixed with pomegranate juice. About halfway to Ajijic, we met the only foreigner we knew of who lived in the area. This man lived somewhere down the road and up in the hills beyond Ajijic. He came along now on a horse, riding in a dignified way because he was a German count. Since Lowelito was of German descent himself, he wanted to greet this count courteously, even though he had never met him formally. So as he approached the count, Lowelito made a sweeping gesture and said, "Good afternoon, Your Highness!" But because of the drink, he fell off his donkey. We had to dismount to help him. The dignified old count did not even stop.

4
El Manglar

Despite all the unrest in Mexico in July, 1926—due to the "Cristero" phase of the Revolution, which was giving the government much trouble—the trains were running on schedule. When President Calles issued his penal code against the Catholic church, just a few days before my departure from Chapala, I was suddenly aware of a great conflict among the people, and I was hoping nothing would happen to prevent my fulfilling my date to meet Eileen up in El Paso. It seemed to me that everybody in Chapala and Ajijic was devoutly religious and on the side of the church, but Alfredo told me that there was also much anti-Catholic feeling in the area. He himself was a devout Catholic. Lowelito and I did not respond one way or the other to this controversy, for we were only interested in our work and in the beauty we were seeing all around us.

Leaving my steamer trunk and art materials in Ajijic, I started my long journey by train. This would be my first trip all the way up to El Paso, which was just across the border from the Mexican city of Juárez. When the slow train finally reached the desert country in northern Mexico, a terrible dust storm started to blow. All the train windows were shut and the weather was very hot. When the train pulled into Juárez, I did not feel at all well. I crossed the border into El Paso and immediately set out to find Eileen, who had come from San Diego. Members of my family had already arrived for the wedding, and borrowing a car from one of them, I drove Eileen out to the edge of the city and placed a modest ring on her finger. I had a raging fever and soon discovered that I was suffering from a strep throat. I believed the hot dust storm must have brought it on.

It took a long week for the fever to abate and for me to recover from the strep throat. If I had been Eileen, I believe I would have given up the whole idea and gone back to San Diego. But fortunately for me, she considered our project worthwhile, and she never wavered. To this day, we do not know how we did it—there were many details to attend to, such as obtaining a marriage license and then finding a minister—but we succeeded in getting married and crossing the border to the Mexican side. Eileen had had to declare her occupation on the Mexican passport, and I was delighted to see her write the word "housewife." A few moments later, when we were on the train, a Mexican nurse came down the aisle demanding proof that everyone had been vaccinated. Eileen told me that she did not want to be vaccinated, since her mother was a Christian Scientist. So, in my innocence, I lent her my own vaccination certificate and was vaccinated myself for the fourth time in about six months. I knew another vaccination would not take

on me, for none had ever taken before. I must have had
a very bad case of smallpox when an infant, I imagined.
But now I had a wife, and little did I know how completely she was to join in all our pursuits.

On the long, hot journey down to Querétaro, where
we would change trains for Guadalajara, Eileen told me
that a person was not "complete" until he had a mate,
that it took two people, a man and a woman, to make
one complete person. I had not realized how incomplete
I had been all those years I had been painting in Mexico. I felt sure my painting was going to be a lot better
when I got back to it.

Eileen didn't speak any Spanish at all. She had stud-
ied French in high school. Although she had lived in a
city close to Mexico, French, not Spanish, was offered in
the schools. But she had picked up a few words in Spanish just from living so close to the border. When we were
in the diner on the train, I heard her say to the Mexican
waiter, "*Por favor, dame un beso de agua.*" Both the Mexican waiter and I were amused, for we knew she wanted
a glass of water. But what she had said was, "Please give
me a water kiss." I told her she might make me jealous if
she weren't more careful with her Spanish.

On that long trip south on the train, Eileen also revealed to me her love of poetry. She introduced me to
the poetry of Edna St. Vincent Millay, and she recited to
me this poem by John Masefield:

I must down to the seas again, to the lonely sea and the
    sky,
And all I ask is a tall ship and a star to steer her by,
And the wheel's kick and the wind's song and the white
    sail's shaking,

Street in Ajijic

Women with Cactus

And a gray mist on the sea's face and a gray dawn
    breaking.

I knew nothing about poetry, but I was surprised to
find that those words of John Masefield conveyed a feeling that was similar to what I had been experiencing in
the subjects I chose to paint. In that street scene in Ajijic, I had seen something that was not at all the same as
what a camera would have caught, and now I knew it
was what I was feeling.

The morning after we had arrived in Guadalajara,
we went out and had breakfast in a little restaurant
called the Copa de Leche. In that little restaurant, I saw
the young Mexican, Javier del Castillo, who had told
Lowelito and me that we should visit Guanajuato. I was
very proud to introduce Eileen to him. I said, "Javier del
Castillo, this is my bride, Eileen."

Javier spoke perfect English, and he said to her in
English, "How do you like Mexico?"

Eileen looked sweetly at him and answered in English, "I am so sorry, but I do not speak Spanish." She
had assumed that since he was Mexican he must surely
be speaking Spanish.

By this time, the little train had stopped going to
Chapala. Why it ceased to operate I never knew, but
once it stopped it never started again. The old station
remained, but the train never returned to it. Eileen and
I went from Guadalajara to Chapala in an old Overland
automobile taxi, and how the driver got us and Eileen's
big trunk over the bad road was almost miraculous. We
went straight to the Mólgora Hotel, which faced the lake
and was right on the plaza. We were greeted there by
Lowelito, Traynham, Isidoro, Alfredo, and Clemente

Mólgora, whose father owned the hotel. That night, Clemente gave an impressive dinner in our honor, with many courses and a different wine with each course. There was much gaiety and many toasts were made. When Eileen and I went to our room in the hotel the walls and the ceiling were spinning. My feet were still some six inches off the floor.

When we went down to breakfast the next morning, we found that the lake was high. The water was right up to the steps of the hotel, and *lirio* (water hyacinth) had been blown over the sidewalks and into the street. But the morning was calm and the sun was shining brightly. The first thing Eileen wanted to do was to go to Ajijic and see the house where we had been living, and also she wanted to see El Manglar, where we would be living as soon as we could move in. I engaged a boatman to take us all to Ajijic in his little outboard motorboat, and we all climbed in. When we started, there was no wind, but as soon as we got out onto the lake and were about halfway to Ajijic, the wind came up so strong that the waves broke over the outboard motor and it conked out. Our boatman had only one oar, and when he tried to steer the boat his oar broke in two pieces. We were then at the mercy of the wind and waves. However, the waves were going toward the near shore, and before lone we drifted into a thicket of tules, where fortunately the water was not over our heads. But since the boat could not get to the shore through the thick tules, we were forced to slide into the water almost up to our necks and wade ashore. We discovered that we were at the village of San Antonio, where the drunken Indians had struggled over the big pistol. We were so cold we went into the first cantina we found in order to warm ourselves with a drink of tequila, the only drink available. The way my twenty-year-old bride tossed down a glass of tequila without a chaser delighted Lowelito, but it was a surprise to me, for at that time I did not know her that well. Eileen had been wearing a bright green dress when we slid into the water, and everything she had on underneath became green and remained green thereafter.

After spending the night in that small Ajijic house, we got another boat to take us back to Chapala the next morning. On the way back, we had the boatman stop at El Manglar, whose pier went out into the lake. That was Eileen's introduction to our honeymoon house. She seemed to be thrilled with it, and with Margarita, our cook. But when she discovered how large the house was, and that there were many rooms, she said to Lowelito and Traynham, "Why don't you both move in with us?"

That was all they wanted to hear. When we arrived at the Mólgora Hotel, Traynham and Lowelito did not even get out of the boat. They immediately started back to Ajijic to get their belongings and move them into El Manglar.

*   *   *

Alfredo had told me that he remembered President Porfirio Díaz's coming to Chapala and staying in El Manglar during the summertime. El Manglar was the last big house on the dirt road leading out of Chapala toward Ajijic, and it was separated from all the other large waterfront houses by at least a quarter of a mile. The distance from it to the plaza in Chapala was about a mile.

In front of the house, a garden with palm trees extended down to a retaining wall at the water's edge, where a pier ran out into the lake. At the end of the pier, stone steps went down into the water.

A wide tile-floored verandah stretched all the way across the front of the house. Behind it, rooms along the front and on two sides enclosed a patio, and at the rear of the patio there was a high wall. Rising up behind it was a great dark grove of mango trees.

Eileen and I took the large music room, with its shining tile floor, for our bedroom. We thought it must have been the old dictator's music room, since it had cupids playing musical instruments painted on the ceiling. It was a very long room, with a big double bed at one end and at the other end a high wardrobe so large that an Indian family could easily have used it as a home.

Traynham chose a room on the road side of the patio, next to the dining room, and Lowelito took a room on that same side but at the very rear, next to the back patio wall. Isidoro, who wanted to live with us, would wrap himself in his red sarape and sleep on the floor just outside our bedroom door. He still preferred the floor to a bed. I was sure he thought of himself as being our guard. The servants slept in the rooms on the other side of the patio. The kitchen was also on that side.

Besides a cook, we had all of Margarita's children, who did the laundry, served table, and kept the house clean. Margarita's husband, who would get drunk at times and stay drunk for a week or so, took care of the garden. His name was Carlos, and we rarely saw him, except at a distance. There were two sons, Carlos, Jr., and Pancho. There were also daughters and possibly nieces. We never knew for sure who was waiting on the table. But regardless of the number of servants we had, we only paid for Margarita and her husband. The others just received their simple board and room.

We had not been settled into El Manglar long before processions started passing our house and going down the dusty road. These processions were made up mostly of women. They all wore dark rebozos over their heads and shoulders, and we soon learned that they were going to the village of San Antonio, where they would pray in the churchyard for the opening of the churches. President Calles's very strong anti-Catholic stance had brought on a boycott in Mexico and caused the Catholic hierarchy to close the churches all over the land. These religious people in Chapala seemed to believe that Calles himself had ordered the churches closed, but the fact was that their closure was the Catholic Church's response to his stringent anticlerical edicts.

One day, we saw a man coming down the road bearing over his shoulder a huge heavy cross, which he was dragging along. On his head, he was wearing a crown of thorns. Apparently this was his way of helping to get the churches to open again. As he came by our gateway, I saw a man stagger up to him and cause him to stop. This second man was obviously very drunk, but his intentions were noble. He persuaded the man with the cross to let him take over, and he even took the crown of thorns and placed it on his own brow. But the two men did not go far down the road before this well-intentioned one began to stagger from one side of the road to the other, and soon he fell to the ground, with the cross over him. The penitent picked up his cross again and proceeded down the road. By that time, the drunken man was fast asleep.

Eileen found these religious processions fascinating. Having been a newspaper reporter, she wanted to write a story about them. So on one occasion she went along with a group of women on their pilgrimage. She told me later that when they all reached the churchyard in San Antonio, all the Indian women started crawling on their hands and knees, while she remained standing alone above them with her raised parasol. That was the first time I noticed the influence of her newspaper background, which I was to observe many times later.

I was eager to get back to my painting, now that I was supposed to be a "complete" person. Directly behind our mango grove was an interesting subject—a group of fishermen's houses with walls made of crude field stones and with straw roofs. The houses seemed to be growing out of the earth, and the people in and around them seemed to be earth people, who looked as though they had been created out of that same earth the houses stood upon.

Eileen said that she would help me carry my easel and paints. That, of course, put Isidoro out of a job. If he was to go on living with us, he needed something to do, so I gave him the steady job of finding Eileen's hairpins each day and presenting them to her each evening. At that time, Eileen had short bobbed hair. She was what the Mexicans called a *pelona*. She used the hairpins to keep her bobbed hair arranged as she believed it should be, and these were forever falling out and getting lost as she walked around. Isidoro now had the job of retrieving them, but before long he made himself useful in other ways as well.

One day I set out with Eileen to paint the fishermen's shacks. To reach them, we had to climb over several of those fences made of stacked-up, uncemented

boulders. After Eileen had helped me get settled to paint, she climbed onto the very top of one of those ancient fences near a shady tree and began to read, while I painted a picture of the houses. Suddenly I heard behind me a rumbling sound, which I first thought might be an earthquake. When I looked around, I saw the rock fence on which Eileen was seated was falling apart. The stones were going down, one after the other, while she remained seated among them. I was frightened that she might get badly hurt, and I sat there helpless. There was nothing I could do. The stones continued to make a rumbling, grinding noise as they kept falling and rolling out onto the flat ground, and Eileen's position was becoming lower and lower in elevation. Finally the noise ceased, and there she was, seated on a big rock in the middle of a whole flat field of stones all laid out over the ground. She had had a most unusual ride, but she was not hurt.

It took me some time to get over my fright and get back to my work, but when my painting was completed I saw that I had recorded a strange relationship among colors that ran from deep dead blacks, through cold grays, to red-browns and vermillions. It seemed to me that I had painted the rock houses the way they were, on their own, free of all outside interpretation.

*   *   *

I had much to learn about this black-haired girl of mine, but she was revealing more of herself to me each day. I soon learned that she was quite socially oriented, and also that she was extremely generous. One evening, she announced to Lowelito and me that we should invite Clemente Mólgora to dinner.

"After all," she said, "he went to lots of trouble and expense putting on that dinner for us when we first arrived in Chapala. We can have Margarita prepare the dinner, you boys can get some wine, and I will bake a cake in that big old cookstove in the kitchen."

I knew that the big iron cooking range probably had not been fired up since old Porfirio Díaz had lived in El Manglar, but I believed Isidoro would know how to do it. Margarita did all of her own cooking with charcoal on one of those shelves like the one Lowelito and I had in the House with the Green Door.

We set a date for the dinner, and Clemente accepted. He would come on his bicycle. Lowelito and Traynham went to the village and chose the wine, and Isidoro went up into the mountains and gathered wild flowers for the table. It was going to be a festive occasion, and also the very first dinner party Eileen would give as a married woman.

When all the arrangements had been made, Eileen announced that she would bake her cake in the kitchen the night before the dinner party. She said it would keep, or even be better after cooling. When we went into the kitchen to discuss the dinner with Margarita and to ask Pancho to get wood and build a fire in the great cookstove, Margarita, the mother of Pancho, explained his condition to us. While she explained, the subject of her story sat there by the cookstove listening with an amused smile on his face. Margarita turned her hand around her ear as though there were a handle projecting from it and said, "*Pancho no tiene nada aquí,*" which meant that he had nothing in his head. "He had a fever when a baby," she explained, "and after that there was nothing remaining in his head."

The cake Eileen started making that night was to be the dessert when Clemente Mólgora came to dinner the next night. Eileen said it was going to be a "layer cake," and that she was going to put mashed bananas between each layer. The stove oven was so roomy that she had all the layers cooking at the same time. But unfortunately she had Pancho open the oven door too soon, and all the cake layers "fell." After the layers were put together, with the bananas in between each one, the whole cake would obviously not be over three inches thick. When Eileen realized this, she began to cry, and my heart was broken because of her disappointment. But luckily I had an inspiration. I said to my bride, "Honey, you do not know what you have done. You have accidentally created a wonderful dessert. It may not be a layer cake, but it will be one of the most beautiful 'Russian omelets' you ever saw."

The next night, the dinner party was a great success. Margarita served a delicious dinner of several courses, the wine was good and plentiful, and Eileen's Russian-omelet dessert was a sensation. Clemente loved it, for it really was delicious. We were all happy over Eileen's dessert. But she was never able to repeat it, for the cakes she made thereafter simply would not fall.

*   *   *

Another one of Eileen's characteristics I soon discovered was that she was a natural-born explorer. I had tramped all over the area around Chapala during the nearly three years I was looking for subjects to paint, and I believed I had pretty well covered it all. But when she started carrying my easel, she began pointing out places I had never thought of visiting. I think the reason was that she refused to be intimidated by difficult places like steep canyons and areas filled with thick brush.

Down the Ajijic road, about a half mile beyond El Manglar, there was a deep and extremely narrow canyon leading back into the mountain. It was completely filled with thick brush, trees, and boulders. It looked impenetrable to me, but to Eileen it was only a splendid challenge. So I followed her into its entrance, and we began struggling over big rocks and around bushes and vines, always going steeply uphill along the sides and near the bottom of the canyon. A stream of water rushing downward caused us to take great care not to fall into it. Finally, Eileen said excitedly, "Listen! I hear water falling!" We continued on toward that sound until we came to a beautiful sight. There before us was a white waterfall, plunging straight down from a ledge about a hundred feet above us, and at the base of the fall we were thrilled to see a clear pool of water almost as large as our El Manglar bedroom. Ferns and trees covered with trumpetlike white flowers were clinging to the sides of the pool, and large rocks were available to sit on near the clear water.

I was now in for another thrill. Eileen began to take off all her clothes, and before I could warn her to be careful she stood there before me like a white forest nymph, and she then plunged into the pool. I soon followed her in, and we had a joyous swim together.

I said to myself, "Eileen has been saving this place for me all this time, until she could join me in Mexico."

We returned to that sylvan pool to swim and bathe once or twice a week after that, and we kept its location a secret. Lowelito and Traynham must have wondered where we were going when we would start down the road, each of us carrying a towel.

*   *   *

Almost every Thursday afternoon, Alfredo Padilla would come to El Manglar for a visit. Sometimes he would arrive with a couple of campesinos, and we would all sit and talk and have a drink on the verandah. Alfredo owned a little drugstore on one of the back streets in Chapala. It was not at all like the drugstore on the corner of the plaza, which belonged to the doctor and catered to the general public. Alfredo's drugstore was for the Indians and other poor people, who came for medicines only when they were sick. In those days we did not know much about Alfredo's past, but we liked him very much. It was years later that I learned how active he had been in politics—that he had known Indians even up in "Los Altos" (the high mountains). I also learned later that he had started out working as a carpenter and as an interpreter, when his father was in charge of building the Chapala railroad station. That station, which stands to this day, was not completed until 1922, only about four years before the railroad itself ceased to operate.

Alfredo had learned to speak English, in his charming Mexican way, and he also knew some Norwegian, which he had learned from a book. The Chapala railroad had been built by a Norwegian company, and since Norwegians worked with his father on the station, Alfredo served as an interpreter as well as a carpenter. He was also a poet.

Lowelito kept saying that we should take Eileen to see Mescala, and that someday we should also take her to see Guanajuato. It had been many months since Lowelito and I were given permission by the Mescala city fathers to live in that village, and since it was Eileen who caused us not to live there, Lowelito said the least we could do was to show her the place. He brought that subject up one Thursday when Alfredo was visiting us, and we set a date to go to Mescala. Like Isidoro, Alfredo insisted that it was a dangerous place, but he was eager to go with us anyway.

We hired a boat to take us there on the date we had agreed upon. There would be only five of us: Lowelito, Alfredo, Isidoro, Eileen, and I. Traynham could not accompany us, for he had promised some Indians to go with them that day to hunt buried treasure.

When our little outboard motorboat docked on the shore in front of Mescala, we had to climb over all of Mescala's rock fences between the shore and the village. Eileen's experience with the falling rock fence had given her no fear of these rock fences, and soon we arrived in the streets of Mescala, which were, as usual, completely deserted. Apparently the people had seen us coming and had gone into their houses. In the plaza, we found a fruit-drink stand with all its equipment in order, but no vendor was in sight. We then went to look at the church and at the large cross in front of it, just as Lowelito, Isidoro, and I had done the year before. Soon a young boy wearing a bright pink shirt came into view. From all appearances, he was the only human survivor in this ghost village. Alfredo asked him if he could get us a bottle of wine, which he was able to do. Later he also knew where to find a pick and shovel for Eileen.

After a while, Isidoro and Eileen started back to the boat with the boy in the pink shirt, while Lowelito, Alfredo, and I remained in the plaza. But it turned out Isidoro and Eileen had not gone more than a block from the plaza when they commenced digging up one of the streets. When Lowelito, Alfredo, and I found them, we saw that they had made a ditch and were now busy putting the cobblestones in a pile. Remembering the Mescalans' lack of enthusiasm for strangers, I was alarmed to see my wife and Isidoro acting so carelessly with the Mescalans' streets by tearing up the cobblestones. My alarm suddenly changed to excitement, however, when I looked into the ditch they had dug, for there, resting like a sleeping person from whom someone had rudely jerked away the blankets, was a skeleton stretched out full length.

The boy in the pink shirt had run off to spread the news. From all the houses, Indians now began to emerge. It was as though someone had rung the fire bell. At last, I was seeing Mescala as a bustling village, with its streets full of people.

At this point, we thought it advisable to withdraw as unobtrusively as possible, leaving the Mescalans with their skeleton. Before we departed, however, we listened to an old Indian woman give her theory regarding the skeleton to the excited crowd of her fellow citizens.

"This poor soul," she said, "was not one of the ancient ones, since there are no *idolos* (idols) buried with him. He was a Christian, and he was killed on this spot during the War of Independence from Spain."

On our return trip to Chapala in the motorboat, I was wondering just how my bride had known where to dig in streets for skeletons. That was a talent of hers I had not expected.

*   *   *

Margarita had assured us that there was nothing in Pancho's head. Nevertheless, he was very helpful, and I preferred to have him run errands for me rather than his younger brother Carlos. Carlos seemed intelligent enough, but one could never tell when he was going to have an epileptic fit. Whenever I would ask Pancho to do something for me, he would do it immediately, even though he would never say a word. He would just smile and then do what I wanted. I began to think that he was not as dumb as Margarita said he was.

One night when Eileen and I were reading in our big bed before blowing all the candles out, Eileen happened to look down on the floor just as a snake was wriggling under the bed. We called Pancho and he came and killed the snake with dispatch. It turned out to be a poisonous one. The next day you could not recognize it, for Pancho had pulverized it into a mass. At intervals during that day, Pancho continued to beat the snake with a big stick. We never asked him why he did that, for we knew he never answered. But in beating on that snake that way, he definitely convinced us that he was weak-minded.

With rock fences falling on her, and poisonous snakes crawling under her bed, I began to fear that Eileen might get fed up with our life in El Manglar. But that was far from the case. She seemed to love every day we were there. The lake also was causing us some trouble, for it had continued to rise until now it was over our pier. Earlier, when the lake was lower, we had often taken baths from that pier, while sitting on the stone steps that led down from the pier into the water. We did have a bathtub in the house, but it was filled with old newspapers and magazines that had been there when we arrived and we had never taken the trouble to remove. Besides, there was no water connected to the tub.

The lake was now in such a flooded state that some of the larger houses on the lakefront had water on their lowest floors. One day, Eileen said to me, "I would like to get some photographs of the flood here. Could you make me a couple of photographs of the flooded houses? Maybe we could row out into the lake in front of those houses and take some pictures of their flooded condition. I think my newspaper would like to have a story about this flood."

I told Eileen that would be no trouble. I would get Traynham to row us by the houses in the rowboat that came with El Manglar, and I would snap the pictures. But when we went out into the lake to take the pictures, Eileen said to me, "Give me the camera." And to my surprise she stood up in the rowboat and pointed the camera not toward the houses along the lakeshore, but toward the open lake.

"This will give a much better idea of the flood here," she said as she handed the camera back to me.

"I am sure it will," I said, "for there is a stretch of water sixty miles long in the direction you were pointing the camera."

But the truth was that she was right. The *lirio* that

was floating on the water next to the houses looked like land. The flood was many times worse than what the pictures of the houses would have shown if she had pointed the camera at the lakeshore. Eileen once again had revealed to me the influence of her newspaper background.

*   *   *

Although we continued to be happy in El Manglar as the months went by so fast, we did not like the continuously rising lake. Besides that annoyance, we were beginning to be entertained by strangers walking about in the house at night. We had so many servants that we would usually assume these unknown people we would meet were members of Margarita's family. But now and then when we met such a person, he would run rapidly out of the house. Sometimes he would even jump off the verandah into the water and keep going. We would know then that he must have been a burglar. This was happening so often that we decided we had better do something about the cash we kept in the house.

In those days there was no paper money in Mexico. So much paper money had been printed by the different generals during the revolution that people simply would not accept it anymore. So all of our money was in silver, which the four of us kept in a small trunk.

One morning at the breakfast table, we discussed this problem. I had brought a little twenty gauge shotgun down to Mexico with me, thinking that I might someday go bird hunting. I now suggested that we put our trunk of silver in one of the bedrooms and let the person who slept in that room keep the shotgun. But Lowelito said he certainly would not shoot anybody, even if the money was being stolen. That let him out as a money guard. Traynham, on the other hand, said that nothing would give him more pleasure than to shoot a thief stealing our money. That statement got him the job.

Traynham's bed had a big mosquito net stretched over a rectangular frame suspended by a cord a few inches from the ceiling. The net hung all the way down on all sides of his bed. Traynham was given the shotgun, which he put under the edge of his mattress on one side of his bed. The trunk with the silver pieces was placed against a wall in his room.

About two o'clock the very next morning, we were all awakened by Traynham yelling at the top of his voice. We ran in to see what was happening, and found him sitting on his bed completely wrapped in the big mosquito net. It had fallen from the ceiling and he had become entangled in it. Traynham told us that he had seen a burglar approaching the door of his room from the patio. The burglar, he said, was silhouetted against the white moonlight outside. The burglar came into the room, but before this intruder reached the bed Traynham pulled the gun from under the mattress. When he swung the gun around, however, the sight on the end of the barrel caught in the net, the string at the ceiling broke, and the whole thing came down on him. The burglar, he said, then ran out into the patio and climbed over the patio wall.

The next morning, we knew Traynham's story was true, for we found that a number of tiles had been dislodged from the wall and had tumbled into the patio.

*   *   *

The water kept rising in the lake until our entire front-yard garden had become a part of the sixty-mile-long lake. The water had not only risen above our retaining wall, but was now threatening to engulf our verandah. Great islands of *lirio* had floated into the area that had formerly been our pretty garden, and we could see snakes among the floating plants. At night, the sound of frogs' croaking filled the air, and I was beginning to wonder when the mosquitos would arrive. To get to the road, we now had to go out the back gate, behind the mango grove.

Several months before, while I was with Eileen in El Paso, Anita Brenner, the writer and art critic, had come to Chapala for a short visit. Lowelito happened to meet her, and she had asked if he would like to work in the Mayan ruins in Yucatán. He told her that he would like that. Now, to his great surprise, he had received an offer to be an "artist in residence" at the ruins of Chichén Itzá, with the Carnegie Institution expedition, under Dr. Sylvanus G. Morley. The expedition would leave Mexico City the following winter. Traynham, although he did not mind the water at all, thought we should move on to Mexico City. Eileen and I knew we would like Mexico City, or any other place. So we all agreed to go there.

Isidoro knew a boatman who had a launch big enough to carry us all, along with our steamer trunks, my roll of paintings—some of which the local postmaster had refused—and Eileen's black suitcase filled with the pre-Columbian figurines she and Isidoro had

dug up. The launch would take us to Ocotlán, at the head of the lake, where we could catch the train to Mexico City. It was agreed that we should leave El Manglar the next morning at daybreak for that long boat ride.

The next day, when the launch had pulled into our yard, now a part of the lake, we were very busy and excited getting everything into the boat. Margarita had cooked a *loma de carne* (meat loaf), which we would take with us for our lunch. As much as we had loved El Manglar, we were now eager to get on to other adventures.

When I had Eileen safely seated in the launch, I said to the others, "All aboard!" And just as I said that, young Carlos started having an epileptic fit. He began jumping up and down, and we had to grab him to keep him from falling off the verandah into the lake.

Everything went smoothly after that. We made connections with the train, checked our baggage, and found seats in the car. Traynham had charge of our large canvas bag filled with silver pesos.

Just as the train started moving, Isidoro ran alongside and handed two parting gifts to Eileen through the train window. They were a little pre-Columbian pot with a face on the rim and a little pre-Columbian animal. We did not know then that many years would go by before we would see Isidoro again.

5
Mexico City

When Lowelito saw me in Ocotlán checking my big steamer trunk, along with the two trunks Eileen had added and also three suitcases, he told me he thought we were making a mistake to acquire so many possessions.

"Possessions will bog you down," he said. "One of these days, you will have to give up traveling, and just stay home and guard your possessions."

Today Eileen and I would not dream of taking so much baggage on a trip, but in those days dragging all those trunks and suitcases along with us did not seem any trouble at all. Everything we did was easy. We made no plans; we did not even make hotel reservations in advance—yet everything fell into place. My older brother used to say that "the Lord always takes care of fools," and it seems clear to me now that He was taking care of us, making all our plans for us.

When Lowelito, Traynham, Eileen, and I arrived in Mexico City from Ocotlán, we went straight to a little Italian hotel Anita Brenner had recommended. It almost seemed that the hotel clerk was expecting us. We checked in, got all our baggage into our rooms, and immediately went out hunting for a house to rent. For some mysterious reason, we went out to the suburb of Coyoacán. There we found just the house we wanted, on Calle de San Pedro. The house was situated only a few blocks from the main plaza, where Cortez was said to have lived after he had conquered the Aztecs in 1521.

Although Coyoacán was a suburb of Mexico City, it was a small village, quiet and restful. It lacked the bustling life of Guanajuato, but it was beautiful in its own way.

We had the good fortune to start living in Mexico City in November, 1926, when it had entered a period of tranquility. Because the period was tranquil and we were on our honeymoon, Eileen and I were seeing everything through rose-colored glasses. But the city was charming at that time, however one looked at it. There were automobiles in the streets then, but not many of them, and of course there was no smog at all. In those days much of the hauling of merchandise was done on the heads of men called *cargadores*, who carried about everything imaginable, from tall bird cages full of birds to heavy tables, chairs, and baskets full of bread.

Mexico City was peaceful when we arrived there that fall, but it had not always been a place of tranquility. During its long history, there were periods when it may have appeared to be having epileptic fits, like Margarita's son Carlos. Carlos too, was calm between seizures. But of all the bad periods in Mexico City, I imagine the worst was the one in 1913, which was brought about by a little Indian general by the name of Victoriano Huerta and a man named Félix Díaz, who was a nephew of the old dictator Porfirio Díaz. Those two had entered into a conspiracy to get rid of Madero, Mexico's elected president. To achieve this, they carried on an artillery duel for ten days within the heart of the city, killing over five thousand people, mostly innocent civilians. Those two generals were not mad at each other at all. They staged that duel simply in order to create chaos before murdering the president and the vice president. During those ten horrible days there surely could not have been a worse place to be than Mexico City. But now all was calm. The revolution that had begun in 1910, originally aimed at overthrowing the old dictator, had about simmered down in 1926, although President Calles and the Catholic church were at great odds. But to Eileen and me, no friction existed anywhere.

In our house at 87 Calle de San Pedro, an unusually long room separated Lowelito and Traynham's bedroom from the bedroom Eileen and I had chosen. It would have taken lots of furniture to fill this long center room, so we decided to leave it unfurnished and to use only its walls. We would hang on its walls all the paintings we were going to paint.

Since the house did not have a stick of furniture in it, not even a table, we had to get some furniture the very first day. We went to the Thieves' Market, where everything was cheap. We bought a dining-room table, a small table for the back porch, two beds, four chairs, and a chest of drawers. All the time we were buying the furniture a *cargador* followed us around to get the job of carrying our purchases to our house. He insisted that he could carry everything, so we gave him the job. We then watched him tie all the furniture together with ropes. After receiving our Coyoacán address, he managed somehow to get under all the furniture and come up with the load on his back. His load extended high into the air, making him almost invisible under it, but he started down the street at a trot. Eileen thought he could never carry it all, but because of my experience with that *cargador* in Guanajuato, I had no doubts about his ability to carry it. I did have some doubt, however, about our ever seeing the furniture again, because of that same *cargador*, who had torn the bottom out of my trunk. But we needn't have worried, for when we arrived at our house a couple of hours later, there was this man waiting for us, with his big load stacked near our entrance door. The distance he had carried it must have been seven or eight miles.

*   *   *

Lowelito did most of his painting in the house, from drawings he made on his walks. But each morning Eileen and I would go out with my box of oil colors and my canvas, stool, and easel. Eileen always carried my easel. Making Eileen my easel carrier insured that she would be with me when I went out to paint. She seemed to like her job, but once I was settled on my stool and had begun to paint, she would wander off and talk to people. In Coyoacán she especially liked to talk to the women who washed clothes along the canal. Often she would return to say that she had found a beautiful sub-

ject for me to paint, perhaps an old stone bridge that spanned the canal at a place where women were washing clothes on rocks. But because Eileen had been writing articles for newspapers since she was twelve years old, everything she was seeing around her in Mexico was exciting material for her writing. Now that we were living in a suburb of Mexico City, she began writing articles about the new "Mexican art renaissance," which was then in full swing. Some of those articles she sold to *The London Studio*, an art magazine in England. For some reason, London seemed closer to us in Mexico City than it had ever seemed back home in the States. I was proud of her for writing those articles, and I would sometimes go with her to get good photographs of Mexican artists' work to illustrate her stories.

We had not been in Coyoacán long when an artist friend of Lowelito's turned up from the States. This young man told us he was an Impressionist. Soon he began tacking up his own paintings on the walls of our unfurnished room. By that time Anita Brenner had introduced us to the artist Jean Charlot, who was a member of the Mexican group of mural painters. Whenever Charlot would drop by to see us, he would go immediately to our long center room to see what we had been painting. We noticed that he would always look carefully at Lowelito's work and also at my work, but that he would pass by the work of the Impressionist as though it simply were not on the walls. Since he apparently had not seen it, although it was in plain view, he would never make any comments about it.

At that time, I think my own painting was also quite impressionistic in style, since I looked at what I painted and tried to record what I believed I was seeing, and since by then I had about ceased "recognizing" the visual subject before me. Perhaps Charlot always looked at my work because I was a friend of Lowelito's, or perhaps because I had such a pretty wife. But Charlot's attitude toward that Impressionist's work made me wonder about the kind of painting I was doing. And when one wonders or questions what he is doing, his faith in his activity is weakened. He may then be very vulnerable to outside influences.

Since those early days, I have continued to be interested in the fact that groups of artists shift from one

style to another quite rapidly, often following some
leader as though they were a flock of sheep, and showing more concern for conformity than for the creation
of visual quality using their own imaginations. Jean
Charlot's attitude toward the painting of that Impressionist may throw some light on the way those shifts
come about. Lowelito and I regarded Charlot with un-
faltering respect, so we watched his responses very carefully. We felt that he just might indicate the right direction to go forward.

In Coyoacán we were so busy painting that there
was not much time left for the discussion of art. Besides,
Lowelito had little respect for ideas. About the only idea
he believed in was that an artist should not think about
painting, but should paint, instead. He said that what we
saw when we looked correctly at things had nothing to
do with ideas, that we were then seeing qualities, not
ideas.

Our great faith in painting was continually being
nourished by the people we were meeting in Mexico
City. They were all hard-working artists, who did not go
to parties often. They thought that art was the most
important thing in the world. We must have caught
their spirit. One day Eileen showed us an *American Mer-
cury* magazine in which there was an article by Joseph
Hergeshiemer. The first sentence in that article said, "I
am getting damn sick of art." We refused to read it, and
felt that it must be sacrilegious.

In Coyoacán we continued the routine we had followed in Chapala. Almost every day, I would go out
painting and Eileen would accompany me. But realizing
there was so much to see in Mexico City, we would take
a day off now and then and go sightseeing. We went to

Chapultepec Park and to Teotihuacán, and we also went to see the mural paintings. Diego Rivera, Orozco, and others were busy painting the walls of public buildings while we were there. Eileen had never seen the murals before, but I had seen some of them when Lowelito and I had stopped off on our way to Guanajuato. Seeing them again, I was surprised to find that the people represented in the paintings seemed to me to be quite true to the people I was seeing in the streets of Mexico City. In fact, the people I was seeing in the streets now looked to me as though they had come right out of the murals. Apparently I had changed, for the figures in the murals certainly did not appear that way to me when I first saw them. But whatever the nature of the change that had taken place in me, it had no effect upon the way I was seeing the subjects I was now painting. I had learned that way of seeing in Chapala and Guanajuato, and now I was applying it in Mexico City.

* * *

When the cook Eileen had found came to work for us, we thought at first she was a spinster. The only name she gave us was "Lupe." But before long she turned up with her little daughter, Luisa, who had blond hair and greenish eyes. The daughter was about six years old, and although she did not have an Indian-like face, she did dress like the Indian children. She was always wrapped in a dark gray rebozo, and she wore pink ribbons on the ends of her braided hair. Lowelito made some drawings of Luisa, and I made a small portrait of her in oils.

One day, Lupe brought along a man whom she introduced as the father of her children. His name was Jesús. The two of them took up residence with us. Behind our kitchen was a bathroom, and in it was a bathtub that was not connected to water and that was completely filled with old newspapers and magazines, exactly as the one at El Manglar. We had been storing some of our suitcases in that unused bathroom. Now Lupe and Jesús would sleep there each night, on a *petate* (straw mat). The room was quite small, and since the bathtub full of old magazines took up so much of the room, I moved Eileen's black suitcase filled with pre-Columbian figurines out onto the back porch. Putting it there proved to be a mistake, but I did learn something from it: I learned that Mexican burglars are not altogether bad.

Lupe had strung up a clothesline between the tall cypress trees in the back yard. One night, while we were sleeping, a thief came over the backyard wall and took all my shirts, which Lupe had drying on the line. He also took the black suitcase with the pre-Columbian figurines. Since we knew the figurines were genuine, having dug them up ourselves, we hated to lose them. A few days later the suitcase filled with the figurines reappeared. Apparently when the burglar opened the suitcase and found that it contained something for which he had no use, he felt obligated to return it to those who might value it.

*   *   *

One afternoon, while I was seated on my stool, painting, Eileen returned from her wanderings and said she had something important to tell me. "Over there," she said excitedly, "at the other side of those vacant lots, I have found a woman who has a cow, a real cow, which she milks! And she will sell us milk if we will bring our own container."

"What are we going to do with all that milk?" I asked her.

"We can have oatmeal for breakfast, for one thing, and Lupe can make us some butter and put a little salt in it for a change. I'm tired of that sweet butter."

I was quite sure that cows in Mexico at that time were never tested for any diseases, and also that milk was not pasteurized. But of course that meant nothing to Eileen, since she had been raised by a Christian Scientist mother. She had even managed to get into Mexico without being vaccinated for smallpox. Lowelito was the same way, although he had never been influenced by Christian Science or any other religion. He made his decisions about what to eat or drink solely on the basis of whether a thing tasted good or not. So, just as I expected, he thought we should take advantage of the cow and start getting its milk.

"I'll go look at the cow," I said. "If she looks all right, I'll ask that woman to sell us milk."

So I went over to see the cow and talk to its owner. I walked across that vacant city block, on the far side of which were some homemade sheds and a small straw house. Great blue-green cactus plants, about ten feet high, were growing all around the place. As I approached, two Mexican women appeared, standing in front of the big nopal cactus plants. They were wearing white blouses and dark red skirts that fell in heavy vertical folds to their bare feet. Their hair was plaited, with white ribbons woven into the braids. They stood so mo-

tionless together that the effect was as if they were posing for me. I stopped and stared at them, and they stood
staring back at me.

When I got over being hypnotized, I went up to
them and said we would like to start getting the milk.
My feeling was that no cow living in such a beautiful setting and having two such exotic milkmaids could possibly give anything but good milk. And that is the way it
turned out. We had that milk regularly after that, and
no one ever got sick. I started a big painting of what I
had seen—those two women standing in front of the
blue-green cactus. When it was finished, I called it simply "Women with Cactus." Years later, it was purchased
by Cliff May, an architectural designer in Los Angeles. I
had prepared my own canvas, which had cracked badly.
The architect, who designed old Spanish-style houses,
especially liked the cracks in my painting, which may
have been the main reason he bought it.

*   *   *

In our wanderings about looking for subjects to
paint that winter, Eileen and I had come to the edge of
El Pedregal (the Stony Place) near San Angel. El Pedregal was the area where, thousands of years before,
lava had settled and cooled after an eruption of the volcano Xitli. The day we discovered El Pedregal, we saw
men working there in a quarry cutting the volcanic
stone into blocks for building materials. The workmen,
in their white *calzones* and red sashes, scattered over the
face of the volcanic cliff made an interesting subject for
painting, so we went there a number of times.

We were told by some of the quarry workers that

baked clay figurines were sometimes found at the base of El Pedregal, which showed that people had been living in the area before the lava rolled over it. Later we learned that under El Pedregal at nearby Copilco there was an old cemetery, which had been excavated. After receiving that information, Eileen said we should go to Tlálpam, where there was an ancient pyramid being excavated by Dr. Byron Cummings, one of her former professors at the University of Arizona. So we went to Tlálpam and tried to find the professor, but unfortunately he was away at the time.

It was in the village of Tlálpam on that day that Eileen saw an old Indian woman with little piles of oranges for sale spread out over a blanket on the ground.

"You buy some," Eileen said. "I can't seem to make her understand me."

"OK," I said. And I went up to the old Indian woman.

"What is the price of your oranges?" I asked her in Spanish.

"Señor," she answered, "those oranges are very sweet, and my price for them is very cheap. I sell each pile of three oranges for twenty centavos. But you can buy one orange for five centavos."

"Well, then," I said, "please sell me one orange." Whereupon, I gave her a five-centavo piece.

"Now," I said, "I would like to buy an orange for my wife," And I gave her five centavos again.

"Señora," I added, "I have a friend who would also like an orange, so please sell me one more." She handed me the last orange in the pile and I paid her five centavos for it.

"Now, señora," I said, "will you please notice that I have all the oranges that composed your pile of oranges, while you received only fifteen centavos for them instead of twenty centavos, which was your price."

The old lady looked at me in what I thought was astonishment from making such a discovery, but it could not have been astonishment, for she said, "Señor, it is clear that what you say is true, but you must remember that you bought the oranges singly instead of the *montón* (the pile), and the price of each orange is five centavos, which explains it all. You should now eat one of the oranges to find how sweet they are."

I thanked her for the oranges, but I also thanked her for teaching me such an interesting lesson in economics.

*   *   *

Lowelito always seemed to have art magazines with reproductions, mostly in black and white, of the paintings currently being created in Paris. He especially liked Matisse, even though he could not tell from the reproductions what colors Matisse had used. I kept noticing that in those magazine reproductions of paintings, buildings were represented as leaning in all directions, almost so far they should fall down. Some of those paintings might have been by Marc Chagall, the Russian painter living in Paris. Lowelito said the buildings were leaning that way because the artist had complete freedom. He said the artist could lean his buildings any way he pleased, because once they got into his painting they belonged to him.

At that time I was having fun discovering what was

actually in the old building walls I was looking at each day, the walls of the old Spanish Colonial architecture in Mexico City. One thing I discovered while trying to paint those old walls was that the color I had formerly seen was a color I had "recognized." It was a color that had a name—like red, or brown—and it was certainly not the color I was now seeing. The color I was now seeing had no name at all, but was more like a force that came right to my eyes and penetrated my entire body. I also found that when I stirred together several different oil colors on my palette, including some white—never mixing them to the point where they became one flat color, but letting each color continue to be visible—the effect was about the same, when the paint was put on the canvas, as that of the old stone walls of the buildings. I called that effect the "quality" of the old walls. The reason I gave that effect a name at all was that I wanted to be sure Eileen understood what I was trying to paint. However, I need not have worried about that, for I soon learned that the color I had recently discovered was the color she had always been seeing.

But while the color I was now seeing was not the color people usually see and consider natural, or "true to nature," the shapes I was seeing remained about the same as those I had formerly seen, which are the shapes I believe people usually recognize. I did not feel it was necessary to change the shapes of the objects I drew in order to get their true visual effect. For me the walls of the buildings did not need to be drawn as though the buildings were about to fall down, the way some of those painters in Paris were drawing them. Up until then, I had never seen any real buildings leaning over so far that they appeared to be on the verge of falling.

One morning Eileen announced that we should take a day off and go and see the Virgin of Guadalupe, on Teypeyac Hill. The story of the Virgin appearing to the Indian Juan Diego several times between December ninth and twelfth in the year 1531 was known to every man, woman, and child in Mexico, and perhaps to Catholics all over the world. Everyone knew that the Virgin had commanded Juan to go see the bishop and have him build a church on that spot, that Juan carried some roses wrapped in his blanket to the bishop, and that when the blanket was spread open there were no roses present but instead a beautiful painting of the Virgin of Guadalupe. A church, or basilica, had then been built in her honor, and that painting was now on view in the church, above the altar. We had heard that between the ninth and the twelfth of December thousands of pilgrims would be coming, so we decided to go there before the crowd arrived.

One cool, clear morning, Lowelito and Eileen and I went out to the village of Guadalupe Hidalgo, where the church was located. We went in a *camión* (bus), because the distance was about nine miles.

When we arrived at the base of the raised plaza, or square, we stepped out of the bus. I looked up and saw before me on the other side of the plaza a large church with towers. It was dark against the light sky—a large, reddish, irregular shape. But what really held my attention was the way the building was leaning over. It was leaning over so far that I felt sure it was about to fall. If only it would stay up a minute or two, I thought, I could call Lowelito. He would see that it was the same as the falling buildings in the Paris paintings. Since he had explained to me why those buildings in the paintings were falling over, perhaps he could now tell me why this real building was leaning so precariously. He and Eileen had walked ahead. They were now up on the raised plaza, walking toward the church calmly as though nothing unusual existed around them.

Suddenly Eileen turned. She and Lowelito were darkly silhouetted against the bright sky, like the dark church ahead of them.

"What on earth is holding you?" she asked. "That's the basilica. Let's go inside and see the Virgin."

But I could not move forward. The leaning building had settled on the retinas of my eyes and had caused me to anchor my feet to the ground and stand rigidly erect. I knew I was holding that building up, and that if I were to move out of my tracks it would begin falling and would crumble to the ground, creating a great noise and sending dust high into the sky.

"You are not going into that building!" I shouted. "It's going to fall any minute now!"

Eileen turned around, and when she noticed that I was anchored in my tracks she came back for me.

"I'm holding that building up!" I said. "You and Lowelito had better not go in. But if you have to," I added, knowing how Eileen liked to explore, "then I'll stay here and hold it up for you."

The basilica did not fall. After all, the Virgin of Guadalupe was inside, and she could hold it without my help. She could hold it up as easily as she could turn roses into her self-portrait. I joined Eileen and Lowelito cautiously. My confidence in the Virgin grew, and the three of us entered the basilica together. As I stood before the altar and gazed up at the painting, I tried to let the Virgin know that I, for one, appreciated the miracle she was performing continuously as she held that great brick edifice together, defying all the laws of gravity. I told her silently that most people who came to see her only admired the miracle she had performed centuries ago, while ignoring the greater one she was performing day in and day out every day of the year. I also thanked her for letting me discover that the visual effect of buildings falling down is far more commanding and exciting than that of buildings balanced and static. Those Paris painters were making good use of their freedom after all.

*   *   *

In the late fall of 1926, the newspapers in Mexico City kept running stories about the "Cristero Revolution," and as we walked along the streets Lowelito, Traynham, Eileen, and I often noticed little placards on doorways and old walls that read, "*Viva Cristo Rey*." But we did not pay much attention to what those stories and placards might mean. We knew that the Catholic Church was very upset by President Calles, but we certainly felt secure living in Coyoacán. So when that Impressionist announced one night that he was "getting the hell out of Mexico because of the revolution," we were both surprised and annoyed. His attitude seemed to us to be uncalled for, and also insulting to our hostess Mexico, for whom we had a great love. We felt that to leave Mexico because she was being threatened by a revolution would be like turning our backs on a friend who was in trouble. But the Impressionist did not feel that way. He took all his impressionistic paintings down from our walls, rolled them up, and wrapped them in old newspapers out of our bathtub. He packed his suitcase, put on his smart topcoat and narrow-brimmed hat, and left for the States. Not long after that Traynham Pitts also departed, but not because he was afraid of a revolution. He had to leave because he was running low on money, and thought he had better get back and find another well-digging job.

Now there would be only three of us living in the house on San Pedro Street, not counting Lupe and Jesús, and Eileen and I knew that Lowelito would be leaving us, too. The time was approaching when he and Jean Charlot were to join Dr. Sylvanus Griswold Morley and go to work in the state of Yucatán. They had both been hired by the Carnegie Institution of Washington, D.C., to make drawings to scale of the ancient Mayan monuments at Chichén Itzá. But Lowelito had been told that in order to work at that archaeological site he would have to own a coat, something he had never owned up to then. Lowelito had always worn a button-up sweater. He was told that Dr. Morley insisted that at the ruins of Chichén Itzá everyone had to wear a coat to dinner each night, that no one could enter the dining room without a coat.

Since Lowelito had to own a coat before he could take the job, and since he had never had any experience with a conventional coat, Eileen thought it was up to her to help him find one.

"I am going to help Lowelito choose a coat," she said. "He wouldn't know whether a coat would fit him or not."

"Just where are you going to find a coat here in Mexico City?" I asked her. "I have never yet seen a dry-goods store here."

At dinner that night, I said to Lowelito, "Eileen will

help you choose a coat all right, but do you know where they sell coats in Mexico City?"

"I don't know," Lowelito answered, "but I suppose in the Thieves' Market. They have everything else there, so they must have coats."

"Of course not the Thieves' Market!" Eileen said. "If they did have coats, they would be secondhand ones. Lowelito doesn't want to go to Yucatán in a secondhand coat! And besides, it probably would have been stolen by some pickpocket."

To that I remarked that I couldn't imagine how a pickpocket could take a whole coat after picking its pockets.

The next morning Eileen and Lowelito left the house early to look for a coat in the city. I was working on my painting of the two women and the cactus, and besides I knew I would be no help in the search for a coat.

They were back a little after noontime. I could see at once that they did not have a coat.

"What happened with the coat?" I asked.

"We went to lots of places," Eileen said, "even to the Thieves' Market. But finally the only place we could get a coat was in a tailor shop, and the tailor was closing his shop for the siesta. He said he would measure Lowelito in the morning and make him a coat. Lowelito is going there in the morning to get measured and to choose the material."

The coat problem seemed to be solved. Lowelito went next day, got measured, and chose the coat material. In a couple of days, when the coat would be finished, Lowelito would be ready to go to Yucatán. He wouldn't be kept out of the Carnegie Institution dining room at the ancient Mayan ruins.

But when he came home one day wearing his new coat, Eileen and I had misgivings. Lowelito had chosen deerskin. It was soft and had a pretty cream color, but the tailor had put a long fringe of deerskin down each sleeve and along the bottom edge of the coat. When Lowelito put on his new deerskin coat, he reminded me of pictures I had seen of Daniel Boone. We did not comment to Lowelito about the fringes, but when we were in our room Eileen mentioned the coat to me and said that she doubted if it would be appropriate. I told her that if Daniel Boone could wear such a coat and get by with it, so could Lowelito.

A short time later, we went to the railroad station one night to see Lowelito off. Charlot was there, and so was Anita Brenner. Everybody was waiting. Finally Dr. Morley arrived. He was wearing an off-white raincoat, but we were disappointed to notice that it had no fringes.

Lowelito boarded the train with all those archaeologists and disappeared. We did not know it then, but we would not see him again for over five years.

*   *   *

Christmas had come and gone. On Christmas day Eileen and I had decided to celebrate the Lord's birthday and also to toast to Lowelito and wish him good luck. First we went to a public bathhouse, where the bathtub was almost as large as a swimming pool. Then we went to Sanborn's for dinner, after which I shocked Eileen by buying a long cigar. I was not a smoker, since smoking got in my way when I was painting, but I thought something special was called for on that day.

The winter kept getting colder and colder. Mexico City can get very cold at that time of year. But it apparently never got cold enough to cause people to put heaters or fireplaces in their houses. When it turned cold, a person was supposed to put on more clothes. But when one is to take a bath, he must of course remove his clothes. Since our bathtub—like most of the bathtubs we had seen in Mexico—was full of old newspapers and not even hooked up to water, Eileen had been taking skimpy sponge baths in our house. But now the house was too cold for such baths, and it was a long way to that place where we had taken a bath on Christmas day. Also, the public baths seemed to me to be undignified, or at least not good enough for my Eileen.

One cold morning, I said to her, "Don't you worry. I am going to fix you a bathtub with warm water and with heat around it."

I went immediately to the Thieves' Market and bought a very large ceramic *cazuela* (casserole). It was about four feet in diameter and at least a foot deep. I took it home and placed in on the floor of our unfurnished room, where now only my own paintings were tacked on the walls.

From then on, whenever Eileen wanted a bath, Lupe would heat water in her pots on the charcoal stove in the kitchen. After the hot water was poured into the *cazuela*, I would make a circle of tall candles all around the bathtub, using dozens of candles, and then as Eileen settled into her bath I would light them all. The lighted candles kept the entire area around her nice and warm. Seated within that brilliant circle of lighted candles, in the nude, she was so beautiful that I almost wished I could have invited the neighbors in to see her. It would also have shown them how they could solve the problem of heating a bathroom—and of taking a bath—in a city whose houses had no built-in heating systems, and whose bathtubs were used for storage purposes.

*   *   *

After Lowelito had disappeared down the railroad track with the archaeologists, we learned that Anita Brenner had had her appendix removed. When we went to see Anita in the hospital I noticed yet another one of Eileen's native characteristics. I discovered that she loved to come to the aid of people who needed help, and that she especially loved to feed them. This generous characteristic caused us to become well acquainted with Anita. When she would be released from the hospital, she would definitely need to recuperate. So Eileen said to her, "You come out and live with us. I will feed you and soon you will be strong again. Our Lupe is a good cook."

I did not know how nice Anita's house was when I heard Eileen extend that invitation, for we had not yet seen it, but I was sure she must have a bed. Since Lowelito had torn up his and Traynham's beds and used the wood to pack his books when he went to Yucatán, we now had only one bed. Lupe and Jesús slept on a straw mat in the bathroom. So another trip to the Thieves' Market was required.

Anita came to our house looking pale, frail, and undernourished, but I knew that condition would not last long with Eileen looking out after her. Soon she was

so strong that she began to pick up the activities her operation had caused her to drop. One project she had
been engaged in was that of helping Ernest Gruening
with a book he was writing on Mexico. Anita and Dr.
Gruening would sit at the little table out on our back
porch and work on the book, *Mexico and its Heritage*.
Later, that author became the governor of Alaska.

Another person who often came to see Anita during her short stay with us was the famous Mexican
painter José Clemente Orozco. If there ever was an artist whose work was like an exploding volcano, it was
Orozco. Yet he had the mildest, gentlest personality of
anyone I had ever known. It seemed incredible to me
that such powerful painting could have been done by
this mild-mannered man. I never really saw his eyes,
which might have revealed his strength. They were hid-
den behind lenses so thick that all one saw were rings of
reflected light.

One day I said to Anita, "Since all these celebrities
are coming out here to see you, Anita, when can we expect a visit from the great Diego Rivera?"

She laughed at this and answered, "That is one person who will not be coming. And neither will his wife,
Lupe Marín, be coming. Neither of them likes me
anymore!"

Anita then explained. "I should have known better," she said. "After all, I was raised in Mexico. But
when I dropped by their home and found Lupe hanging from the top of the door while Diego was wham-
ming her backsides with a big thick board, I couldn't
keep out of it. I rushed right in to stop his cruel treat-
ment of his wife. And you may not believe what happened. They both turned on me, especially Lupe, and I

was lucky to get out of the house unharmed. Neither of them has spoken to me since, and they both were my good friends."

Charlot was also a good friend of Anita's. It was even rumored that they might have gotten married had it not been for their different religions. Anita was Jewish, while Charlot was a devout Catholic.

Lowelito also admired Anita very much. She was a brilliant, sensitive person, with a mind capable of entertaining anything as possible. She even believed that there might be a world of spirits capable of coming back to earth and moving things around physically. In those days, Sir Arthur Conan Doyle was writing and lecturing on the subject of spiritualism, and Anita seemed inclined to believe what he said. But Eileen couldn't go along with her on that. Eileen is Irish, but she doesn't allow spirits to come into the house and break the dishes.

"I don't think they will ever do it," Eileen said. "I don't think they can do it. If they exist at all, they don't have the power to come in and break the dishes."

"That's just what you think!" replied Anita. "You are just the kind of person who might have said that there was no such thing as electricity!"

* * *

Anita had described the beauty of Tehuantepec to us, and had said that I should, by all means, do some painting down there. After she became strong again and could walk as well as ever, she left us and returned to her own home. Eileen and I returned to our daily walks with my painting equipment, but now we could think of nothing else but Tehuantepec.

One afternoon, when we arrived back at our house on San Pedro, only Lupe was there. She said that Jesús—who, it had turned out, was not her husband, as we had assumed, but her husband-to-be—was mad at her. He had gone away, she said, because she had told him that it was high time he married her. After all, they now had two children who were old enough to be going to school. I told Lupe I would speak to Jesús as soon as he came back, and that I was sure he would come back.

Our house seemed very large now that Lowelito, Traynham, and that Impressionist had gone away. The center room looked especially long and bare, for I had taken my own paintings—which were all that were left after Lowelito and the Impressionist had taken theirs—and carried them to the Mexico City post office. I was able to mail them back to the States without any difficulty, since, as it turned out, the postal clerk in that office happened not to be an art critic.

One day, we received a note from Anita Brenner inviting us to her house for dinner. She said that she herself was going to cook a turkey. We did not know why she had decided on a turkey, since it was so long after Christmas, but Eileen was delighted to think that we were going to have real baked turkey, American-style food for a change. I said I hoped Anita also knew how to make good dressing to go in the turkey.

We arrived at Anita's house right on time, about one in the afternoon. In Mexico City, people had their main meal at midday instead of at night. The interior of Anita's house seemed quite dark. There was a fairly strong odor of Mexican food in the air, and I began to fear that Anita had changed her mind and was going to serve us enchiladas instead of good old American turkey.

We were her only guests, and she was her own cook. She invited us to be seated. "Now," she announced, "I bring in the pièce de résistance, the turkey." She then emerged from the kitchen carrying on a large plate what surely had the shape of a turkey, but it was as black as my shoe. I wanted to assure Eileen not to worry, that Anita had obviously baked the turkey in mud. I had heard of baking things in mud, but had never seen it done before. But this mud, I had to admit to myself, had a strong peppery odor.

"You are going to love this turkey!" Anita enthused. "I have baked it in *mole*. You start carving, Everett. I have lots more *mole* in the kitchen!"

People who have never had turkey or chicken in *mole poblano* usually do not like it the first time they try it. It is a dish for which one must develop a taste, and we had never even seen it before. We found it hard to take, and it was even harder to pretend that we were enjoying it. But I believe Anita never knew how disappointed we were. That black turkey did not fulfill our expectations at all.

On the way back to our house, I told Eileen that I would bake a turkey myself as soon as we got settled in Tehuantepec. I also assured her that the *mole* flavor of Anita's turkey would help prevent us from catching any tropical diseases down in the banana country.

"Well, then," Eileen said, "let's get down there as soon as possible."

"I know *mole* must be good medicine," I added, "but I will feel a lot safer if you will let me get you vaccinated before we go. Everywhere I look in Mexico, I see people with pock-marked faces—especially their noses—and I don't want that to happen to your pretty face."

A few days later, Jesús returned to Lupe. I was not surprised he had come back, but I was surprised that he had sent Lupe to ask if he might speak with me, since he usually kept out of my sight. To make Lupe feel better, I had told her that I would speak to her husband-to-be and tell him I did not think Lupe had insulted him by suggesting that they get married. Now, it was her husband-to-be who wanted to talk to me.

I went back to the bathroom, where Lupe and Jesús lived, to see what he wanted to talk to me about. I found him reclining on top of all the old newspapers and magazines in the bathtub. When I entered, he jumped to his feet.

"Señor," he began, "I have been deeply troubled for some time, ever since Lupe started working for you here."

"Don't you want Lupe to work for us?" I asked.

"Yes, Señor, I want her to work for you, but ever since she came here she has been asking me to marry with her. Every day, she asks me the embarrassing question, 'Just when are you going to marry with me?'"

I asked Jesús what was wrong in her wishing to be married.

"I do not object to marrying with Lupe," he replied. "And that is why I wanted to speak with you. Do you not think this constant nagging me to marry with her is a sign that she no longer loves me?"

"Jesús," I said, "I am sure you are mistaken about that. I am sure Lupe loves you more than ever. Perhaps living here with my wife and me has given her the idea that it would be well to be married to you. Jesús," I continued, "my wife and I will be leaving soon, and when we go we want to give you and Lupe all our furniture, everything we bought in the Thieves' Market. The beds, the two tables, all the chairs will belong to you and Lupe."

During the next ten days, there was no break in our routine. We continued living in Coyoacán as though we were not about to leave for southern Mexico. It was as though our big trunks packed themselves. And when the time arrived, those trunks got themselves to the railroad station and got checked to Tehuantepec, by way of Veracruz, Córdoba, and Juchitán. Eileen did not get vaccinated for smallpox, because the doctor could never seem to find any fresh vaccine. However, I did find some capsules of quinine, which we began to take regularly. Later we learned that there was no use taking quinine as a preventive for malaria. Apparently it works only after the disease has set in.

Lupe and Jesús were always together during that time. They were always smiling and laughing. Jesús was constantly in the kitchen helping Lupe with the cooking and dish washing. He had become a devoted husband, completely lacking in machismo, ever since they had succeeded in finding a padre to marry them, even though all the churches were still closed. Eileen and I were delighted to learn that their children had attended the wedding ceremony.

As we left our house on San Pedro one morning for the railroad station, never to see those two again, they seemed sad to see us leave. They thanked us for the furniture we had given them, and wished that we both would go with God on our journey south.

6
Tehuantepec

When our train reached Veracruz, on its way from Mexico City to Tehuantepec, Eileen and I decided to get off and visit that seaport for a few days. But while we were there something happened which made us think that nature, or perhaps some Indian god, was trying to keep us out of southern Mexico. When we stopped over in Veracruz, Eileen's face suddenly swelled up and became as round as the full moon. While I did not dislike the way she looked, I knew that something should be done about it so I got a Mexican doctor to come and see her at our hotel. He gave her an injection, and her face almost immediately went back to normal. To this day, we do not know what caused it, and she has never been moon-faced since.

Anita Brenner had told us so much about Tehuan-tepec, and also Oaxaca, that we were determined to visit both places. We decided to go to Tehuantepec first, and stop off in Oaxaca on our return north.

Although the train we took south from Veracruz was slow and stopped at every village along the way, we soon realized that it was taking us deep into southern Mexico. We rode for miles and miles through vast fields of banana trees that stretched as far as the eye could see. It seemed to us that Mexico surely must supply the whole world with bananas. Our train crossed great tropical rivers and entered new fields of banana trees on the far side. And the farther south we went, the hotter the weather became, even though it was in the middle of January. In those days trains did not have air conditioning. But despite our discomfort, we were happy, especially because we knew that our destination—the old city of Tehuantepec—was some sort of paradise. Anita had assured us of that.

Finally after several days of tiresome travel and after transferring to another train at a town then called San Gerónimo and now called Ixtepec, we were going through more banana fields when suddenly the train began to slow down and came to a stop. After a violent jerk backward, then a violent jerk forward, it seemed to shiver from one end to the other.

I said to Eileen, "I wonder what we are stopping here for?"

She looked out the window and answered, "We are stopping here because we have arrived in Tehuantepec. It says so on the station."

We were in Tehuantepec, all right, and it was such a flat place and so surrounded by a sea of banana and co-conut trees that it could barely be seen.

We got off the train with our suitcases and were surprised no boys were present to fight over carrying our bags. It was obvious that no one was expecting us or caring whether we were in Tehuantepec or not. We had to walk into town carrying our bags ourselves.

On the main street, near the plaza, we found a small hotel and settled into a little room that had a window opening onto a side street. We were interested and somewhat surprised to learn from the hotel clerk that the artist Miguel Covarrubias and his wife, Rose, had just vacated the room assigned to us.

If Tehuantepec was a paradise, as we had been led to believe, we had not seen any evidence of it so far. The only thing there that had interested me as a painter was the sight of dozens of red-headed buzzards sitting in treetops around the town. I had not painted any buzzards up to that time, but I was thinking that now might be a good time to start.

We did not stay long in the little hotel, but almost immediately began searching for a private place where I would be able to paint without being distracted by the general public. Less than two blocks from the hotel, we found just what we wanted. It was a large, low *casa de huéspedes*, with a central patio surrounded by rooms, and with a covered porch around three sides of the patio. Eileen and I rented a large room right across the patio from a bathroom that had an overhead shower. The water for the shower was stored in a metal tank on the roof, where it was kept very warm by the hot tropical sun. We soon learned that in such a hot country a warm shower makes one feel better than a cold shower. The house we would now live in was run by a nice old mestizo woman, who served us good food, including fried beans as the last course of every meal. The beans came in a small roll, and since they were jet black as well as rolled, the dish looked as though it carried a cigar. But we found the fried black beans delicious and were glad that they were served at all meals.

When we began to explore the town, we were struck by how low all the buildings were. We were told that this was because of frequent and violent earthquakes. The squat churches looked especially odd to us. But what fascinated us most were the native women, once they came out of their houses and into the streets from their siestas. They were not only beautiful but also dressed in a colorful type of costume with long white fluted folds at the lower part of the dresses. Some of the women had quite fair skin, although most of them were pure Indian types. The men of Tehuantepec were completely inconspicuous, mainly because they left the town each morning early to work in the fields, leaving the women to run the town and the market.

I could see at once that I would not have to stoop to painting buzzards in Tehuantepec if only I could get some of the Tehuanas (Tehuantepec women) to pose for me. I was also beginning to understand what Anita meant by her enthusiastic description of the place.

All the Tehuanas wore strings of gold coins around their necks, long necklaces consisting of U.S. gold pieces and the large fifty-peso coins called *centenarios*. And some of the women, when they smiled, showed a row of gold front teeth. We did not find that attractive, but apparently they considered their beauty enhanced by the gold teeth. I was glad only a few of them had this additional attraction. All the Tehuantepec women were merchants to their very teeth, and I imagined they put their profits into gold necklaces instead of taking their money to the bank.

Eileen and I began taking walks all over the old city, which, before the arrival of the Spaniards, was the capital of the Zapotec Indian kingdom. The Zapotec Indians, still speaking their ancient language, had continued to live in Tehuantepec. We seldom heard Spanish spoken there. Along the southern edge of the town flowed the wide Tehuantepec River. When we walked over to it, we were delighted to find the beautiful Tehuanas, some nude to the waist, others completely nude, washing their clothes and taking dips in the water along the sandy shore. A long steel railroad bridge spanned the river for the train that went on to the Pacific Coast town of Salina Cruz, only a few miles away. We noticed that the natives were continuously crossing the train bridge, going back and forth on foot.

But before I had contacted any Tehuanas to pose for me in our room, I had, on one of our walks, come upon a tree so large and so fantastic that I knew I would have to make a painting of it first of all. We had discovered that tree while walking during the middle of the hot day, when all the people were inside taking their siestas. Not a person was in sight, only the giant tree with its tremendous trunk and limbs, which formed a complex, tangible structure cutting in all directions through the hot space. Large yellow-green leaves were suspended like dinner plates from the ends of the limbs. The tree was so large its limbs extended across the entire street and spread over the nearby houses. Blue shadows were scattered over the ground, competing with brilliant shapes of white sunlight, and the hot space around the great tree trunk and between the elephantlike limbs

appeared to be vibrating with some invisible kind of energy. I came back at that same time of day until I finished my painting, which was never seen by the natives, who were always sleeping in their houses while I worked. It was so hot there in the middle of the day that I insisted Eileen remain in our room while I painted.

One day, when I had returned to our boarding-house and was cleaning my palette in the patio, a young red-headed American man came walking in.

"I am Abel," he said. "I am Anita Brenner's nephew."

Eileen and I were pleased to meet this serious young man, who immediately began to give us disturbing information.

"You should not walk around the town freely," he said. "You will surely be kidnapped."

We told him that we were intending to walk over the railroad bridge and on to Salina Cruz someday soon.

"Do not do that," he warned. "This is a dangerous place, and you will surely be kidnapped and held for ransom."

*   *   *

Shortly after I had painted the great tree, which I believe was a cotton-silk tree, Eileen succeeded in lining up some Tehuanas for me to draw and paint in our room. She can make herself understood in any language, whether she speaks it or not. Zapotec was no problem for her, even though she did not know one word of that language. I made a number of drawings and small paintings of the Tehuanas, and from the understanding I got of their form and costumes, I began making figure compositions of them. I had also observed the men in the fields wearing their white *calzones* and small high-crowned hats, so I made some compositions of them, too.

After I had worked indoors for a week or so we started walking again. Eileen always wants to see what is around the next corner or over the next hill, so, following her suggestions, we began to walk farther and farther out into the banana and coconut groves. The trails that led through the groves were very narrow, just wide enough for an oxcart. We would often meet these carts being pulled by great oxen, and we would have to move out of the lane into the banana plants to let the carts go by. One day on one of our walks deep into the banana groves, we suddenly came to an open field where all the banana trees and coconut trees had been cleared away

over an area of about one hundred yards square. This open field was surrounded by a dense wall of banana and coconut trees, and at one end we saw a low house with a red tile roof.

"I see some people over there," Eileen said. "I'm going over and talk with them."

I told her they were probably Zapotecs like everyone else and that she wouldn't get very far with her conversation, but she made a beeline for that house, arriving there ahead of me.

As I had expected, the people were Zapotec Indians, who could not speak any Spanish. But nevertheless, Eileen had made contact. An old woman, sitting in a hog-skin chair, with Eileen beside her, was giving orders to a young Indian boy as he stood before her with a machete in his hand. The boy ran toward the far side of the field, and we watched him start climbing a coconut tree. Although the tree was very tall and steep, he was going up fast. He had a rope tied around his body and also around the tree trunk, and he seemed to be shoving the rope up ahead of him as he climbed. We watched him cut several large green coconuts and let them fall to the ground. Then he quickly came down the trunk himself. Eileen was still conversing with the old Zapotec woman when the boy arrived with the green coconuts. With his machete, he sliced the top off each coconut and passed them around to us all. The coconut water was refreshing, and, to my surprise, very cool as well.

Eileen told me that the old woman had told her that if we would drink only the water from the green coconuts we would never get malaria.

On our return that afternoon, I noticed a barbershop on one of the streets. I announced to Eileen that I was going to get a shave in that shop the very next day. "I think it will be interesting to get a haircut and shave in this Zapotec town," I said.

The barber who worked in that shop must have been a pure Zapotec Indian. When I arrived there the next day, I found that he spoke no Spanish at all, and I thought to myself that this would be one haircut in my life which would take place in complete silence. By using Eileen's method of communication, I was able to let the barber know that I would like to have a shave and a haircut. But when I climbed into his primitive barber chair and noticed that he was going to give me the shave first, I imagined he had not understood that I also wanted a haircut, since that is usually done before the shave. I soon learned that I was about to get an old traditional Indian shave, one that might have been considered a kind of Indian sacrifice.

The barbershop opened directly onto the street and was without doors, so there were lots of flies inside. The Indian barber had adopted modern tools. His razor was of steel rather than of flint, and he used soap, although I was sure that he had made it himself, for it was in large, triangular cuts like cheese and looked like the kind I remembered from my childhood, made at hog-killing time in the South.

As he lathered my face with this soap, he used what was recognizably a brush, but had it not been for my own Indian qualities, picked up from Isidoro and Alfredo, it would have been better had he first tied me securely into his chair. The soap burned frightfully. However, that was but a minor inconvenience. What was much worse was the bursting of the soap bubbles and the ravenous appetite of the flies for the soap. All the while, the barber showed no sign of being aware of my plight, and I am proud that I gave him no reason to. Yet secretly I think we both knew that the whole procedure was necessary in order that the earth would remain fertile and the gods be pleased to allow us Zapotecs to go on thriving under Mexican rule.

When I was finally released from the Zapotec Indian's barber chair, my face stinging frightfully, I walked home by way of the marketplace, where I purchased from a Zapotec businesswoman several large green coconuts. I was determined that Eileen and I should drink nothing but coconut water for the rest of our stay in

Tehuantepec. We had continued the precaution of taking quinine every day, believing it would keep the malaria from striking us.

It was very hot as I walked toward our house with
my straw bag of coconuts. My face seemed to be on fire
from the Indian shave, and I noticed that I was a bit
dizzy. But as I approached the house I began to get
cold. Despite the great heat of the day, my teeth were
chattering. The climate seemed to have changed suddenly to freezing temperature. I must have looked sick
when I entered our room, for Eileen came running toward me and helped get me into bed. I was shivering all
over by then. Eileen immediately began to pile bed-
clothes onto me and even clothes out of the clothes
closet. Since I was still shaking violently, she climbed on
top of the pile, trying to get me warm.

When finally the chill subsided, I seemed to be burn-
ing with fever again. Leaving a tall glass of coconut
water by my bed and looking frightened, Eileen announced that she was going to search for a doctor.

I do not know how she did it, but she came back
soon with a genuine doctor. He was a Japanese doctor
who had retired to a large banana plantation, but Eileen
had succeeded in getting him back into the medicine
business. He proceeded to heat water to sterilize his
large hypodermic needle. Then he thumped my chest
and injected a large quantity of quinine into my hip. In
a short time, the quinine caused my chills and fever to
cease. When the doctor returned the next day, he told
us we should leave the tropics immediately or I might
get tuberculosis. Speaking perfect English, he told me
that in about fifteen or twenty years the United States of
America and Japan would be at war with each other.

That prediction caused me to recall that some years earlier, while I was attending Texas A&M College, a military school, I had heard a United States Army general say the same thing. I was now inclined to suspect that there might be a class of people in the world that knew what the future held for the rest of us.

Eileen took the Japanese doctor's advice about leaving the tropics very seriously. I had lost weight and felt very tired, but she thought we should leave right away. She almost carried me down to the station, where we took the train that would carry us out of the Mexico we loved and into the land of our birth and citizenship.

But our trip north did not go as rapidly as we had hoped. Somewhere behind us, the large steamer trunks we had checked from Tehuantepec seemed to be loitering along the way. When we reached the old town of Córdoba, we thought it advisable to wait until the trunks caught up with us, so we checked into a little hotel there. In the streets of Córdoba, we ran into a noisy anti-American demonstration. The banners and placards the marchers carried seemed to express such hatred for Wall Street and gringos that I advised Eileen not to speak any English. I told her to speak to me in her unique brand of Spanish and if anyone asked her what her nationality was to say she was Swiss. She had been mistaken for being Swiss in Mexico City. We had to remain in Córdoba four days before our trunks arrived, but nothing unpleasant happened. The Mexican people do not dislike individuals; they only dislike certain ideas that are associated with them.

On the long, slow trip up toward the border, I kept thinking of the old black suitcase full of pre-Columbian figurines we had shipped up to the States from Mexico

City. I wanted to study those little clay figures carefully, for I had come to believe that each of them held a statement from the distant past, and that there must be a way to understand that statement. I had been impressed to see how alive the figurines appeared to be when Eileen and Isidoro first dug them from the soil back of Chapala. They were so different from the dry pieces of off-white human bone found with them. It seemed to me that the bone had nothing to say beyond its physical existence, while the little figurines were alive and talking. All one needed was to know their language. I believed the same was true of the art, the artifacts, and the architecture of the high cultures of ancient Mexico—of the Mayas, the Zapotecs, the Mixtecs, the Olmecs, and all the others. The thought also came to me that the way to learn the language these ancient objects were speaking was to draw and paint them in a completely objective way.

Such thoughts as these obsessed me as the train carried us closer and closer to the exit gate from Mexico. There was only one way I could dispel the sadness that came over me at the thought of leaving all this behind, and that was to be determined to return. My search had only just begun.

The ringing in my ears from the quinine was with me when I said to Eileen, "We must come back. We must not let the mosquitos keep us out of Mexico forever. What do you think?"

Eileen gave me a sad look that seemed to mean she had understood all I had been thinking.

"You will return," she said, "but don't forget, I will be with you when you do."